S

THE STORY OF KING SAUL AND KING DAVID

THE STORY

·OF·

KING SAUL

·AND·

KING DAVID

LORE SEGAL

Illustrated with 40 reproductions from the Pamplona Bibles

SCHOCKEN BOOKS · NEW YORK

Grateful acknowledgment is made to the Municipal
Library of Amiens (France) and the University Library
of Augsburg (Germany) for permission to reproduce
illustrations from the Pamplona Bibles. (See List of
Illustrations, page ix.)

Library of Congress Cataloging-in-Publication Data

Segal, Lore Groszmann.
    The story of King Saul and King David / Lore
Segal.
        p.   cm.
    Summary: The Bible story is illustrated with
reproductions from the Pamplona Bibles, two
thirteenth-century illuminated manuscripts.
    1. Saul, King of Israel—Juvenile literature.
2. David, King of Israel—Juvenile literature.
3. Bible. O.T.—Biography—Juvenile literature.
4. Bible stories, English—O.T. Samuel.
[1. Saul, King of Israel.   2. David, King of
Israel.   3. Bible stories—O.T.]
I. Title.
BS580.S3S44   1991
222'.4305209—dc20   90-52544

ISBN 0-8052-4088-8

Book Design by Guenet Abraham

Manufactured in the United States of America

First Edition

CONTENTS

LIST OF ILLUSTRATIONS

Illustrations in this book are reproduced from the Pamplona Bibles, two thirteenth-century picture Bibles commissioned by King Sancho el Fuerte of Navarra (1194–1234). The original manuscripts are housed at the *Bibliotheque Municipale d'Amiens* (Amiens Manuscript Latin 108) and *Universitätsbibliothek Augsburg* (Harburg Ms. 1, 2, lat. 4°, 15). The Publishers wish to thank these two institutions for their kind assistance and permission to reproduce this art.

PREFACE

The Story of King Saul and King David is a new translation of I Samuel and II Samuel and the beginning of I Kings. It tells the events of the lives and reigns of the first two kings of Israel.

Did writers make it up, or is it a history of things that happened, or do we think of it as sacred text? Can we think of it as all three?

As sacred text, the Bible chronicles God's plan for the world that He has created in the Book of Genesis—a very good world it was until He formed Adam and Eve out of dust and spirit and gave them the option to disobey Him. Genesis goes on to tell the story of a world grown so evil that God sends a flood to drown everything that He has made so that He can start from scratch—a vain hope, God knows: He places His rainbow in the sky to seal His first covenant with humankind promising never to try that again, for we always were and are always going to be wicked and violent. God frustrates the ambitious technology of the Tower of Babel by inventing a diversity of languages and creating nations which He scatters over the face of the earth. And now the story pans down onto Haran, the center of the ancient world's civilization, and focuses on the family of Abraham.

Abraham is a direct descendant of Adam, and God has elected him to father His special nation, the Hebrews, who will also come to be known as the children of Israel. He tells

Abraham to go west to the land of Canaan, which will come to be known as Israel, the promised land flowing with milk and honey and a lot of trouble. And it will take hundreds of years and there will be a lot of wickedness and violence until we get there.

Genesis tells the stories of the patriarchs, Abraham, Isaac, and Jacob, their wives and children, their households of servants and their great herds of cattle living in a land of strangers. The Lord repeats His promise of their great expectations.

Our forefathers and mothers live lives full of miracles and ordinariness: men must find wives from among their cousins back in Haran, love some and not others; women grieve and worry over their childlessness; parents have favorites. Brothers struggle with each other for their birthright; there's an uncle who cheats a nephew; a sister who is raped and her brothers brutally avenge her. When famine strikes, the men take their families to sojourn down in Egypt and are not above lying to save their skins and enhance their wealth in gold, silver, and cattle.

But whether or not our forebears behave as we would prescribe for them, they're never out of touch with the Lord. He is immanent in their sorrows and worries: He sends messages via visiting angels to foretell births to the barren women, and it is He who determines which brother shall inherit his father's blessing. He commands Abraham to sacrifice his beloved heir Isaac and then prevents him. He raises Jacob's ladder between earth and heaven and wrestles with him through the night. The Lord uses our forefathers' good faith and their bad behavior equally for His own purposes: it is Joseph's tendency to tattle and dream grandiose dreams for which his brothers sell him into Egypt so that he can acquire the power that will preserve the Egyptians from the effect of the great famine and save his father and these same brothers—the progenitors of the twelve tribes of Israel.

I recall the children's book called *Fortunately, Unfortunately*: unfortunately, a later pharaoh enslaves the children of Israel for four hundred years; fortunately, the Lord sends Moses to lead them out of Egypt. Unfortunately, that whole generation, including Moses, disobeys the Lord and must die out during their forty-year trek through the wilderness; fortunately, Joshua will lead their children across the Jordan into Canaan and rout the inhabitants, but there will unfortunately always be enough of them to tempt the Lord's people into the worship of false gods for which the Lord will punish them by handing them over to the enemy's power. Fortunately, he gives them judges to judge and govern and lead them to victory.

■ ■

HERE is where the first book of Samuel takes up the story of another childless woman. Hannah asks the Lord for a son, and the Lord gives her Samuel, whom she gives to the Lord's service. It is a time when the dialogue between God and His people Israel is at a low, and even the sons of Eli the priest are a wicked lot. The Philistines are in the ascendant. The people ask the unwilling prophet Samuel to give them a human king to lead them in their wars against the enemy nations, all of whom have kings. Perhaps the children of Israel remember the early days in the wilderness when the Lord used to move in front of them—a pillar of cloud their eyes could see by day and a column of light by night. The Lord tells Samuel to anoint young Saul.

God's chronicle works itself out in terms of human history. Government by monarchy is put to many tests. Sometimes the Israelites rout the Philistines and the other enemies that surround them on all sides; sometimes Israel is routed. We learn of the movements of armies, of encampments, battle plans, and sieges.

There are periods of peace when we are given the names of the cabinet that runs the state. There are always domestic problems to be dealt with—plagues and more famines. There's the ongoing civil war between the northern kingdom of Israel that remains loyal to the house of Saul and the southern kingdom of Judah that will elect to follow the new king David.

Kings have human natures, commanders have private lives, loyalties, ambitions, and vendettas that change the course of public events. Let us marvel at the writers of our Bible. They have not written about cardboard heroes but about men and women as complicated as the people we are and the people we know. We have to watch the characters in the story and see what they do and hear what they are saying if we want to understand what kind of people they are and to speculate about what they might be feeling and what they might have in mind.

Observe Saul, a tall, beautiful young man, so shy that after he's elected king his subjects have to go and get him out from behind the baggage where he's hiding. You can understand why there are people who laugh and can't imagine that this is the fellow who's going to save Israel from the Philistines. But Saul is roused to a sacred rage when the brutal enemy threatens to humiliate Israel by gouging out the eyes of the besieged citizens of Jabesh-gilead. The young king saves the city and catapults himself into royal power.

Unfortunately, he makes several mistakes, or rather makes the same mistake twice: he doesn't do what the Lord tells him—he doesn't wait when told to wait, doesn't kill all the Amalekites he has been told to massacre. The word comes to Samuel to go and anoint David to be king in Saul's stead.

There is nothing in our literature more painful than to watch Saul watching his destiny slip out of his grasp. Everything—his prowess as a warrior, the love of his people, his own son's affections, pass to young David: Saul has lost the Lord's favor; David has gained it. Saul's sanity slips and his terror can be assuaged only by the harp played by the very David who is destined to disinherit him. We can feel Saul's pain as he sits under a tree, spear in hand, accusing his men of being in league with David, of their lack of love, of their lack of pity because they won't tell him of his enemies' whereabouts.

And all the while Saul knows David is innocent, knows David will be king, and he never stops loving and never stops hating and never stops hunting and meaning to kill his young protégé.

If Saul is one of the most tragic figures in the world's literature, David is the most brilliant. Everybody loves David—God, the court, the army, the people, the king who is out for his life. His best friend is King Saul's son Jonathan, whom he will displace as the royal heir. Everyone who stands in the line of succession is killed for David without his collusion: he has the luxury of punishing the regicides and singing beautiful laments over his dead rivals before he ascends their throne with everybody's blessings. A simpler fiction would have asked us to think David either a politician or a saint, but our subtle story shows us a David who is lucky by the grace of God.

David plays more roles, in more situations, than the protagonist of any modern novel. He is the romantic boy warrior who kills the enemy's giant champion Goliath with a stone out of a brook, slung from a slingshot. David is the musician who can soothe evil spirits, the poet who composes dirges and psalms. He is the innocent victim of the mad king's murderous rage who is forced to exile himself in the land of the enemy, where he becomes the leader of a group of discontents and marauders that massacres the host's cities. We'll see David as king, general, diplomat, a natural at public relations, and as private man. As a boy David annoys his older brother; as a son he takes care of his parents' safety. He is a loving friend who is faithful to his promises. He has a palace full of wives and concubines. As a father he sees his sons rape, murder, raise up an insurrection, and plan his death. When they die, he howls with grief. Nor does the story hesitate to show us also our hero-king as an adulterer who plots the murder of his mistress's husband, is reprimanded by God's prophet, and has the grace to acknowledge his sin. He is human and turns into an old man, who meets a new Goliath and can't do anything about it, can't make love, can't keep himself warm, and passes the kingdom on to his son, the great King Solomon.

■ ■

A WORD about our translation: *The Story of King Saul and King David* gratefully avails itself of modern scholarship, particularly the Anchor Bible, as well as old and modern Bible translations—the German of Luther, the King James, and the Jewish Publication Society's translation.

The Samuel texts are peculiarly difficult. They exist not in original manuscript but in copies incorporating scribes' errors often recopied, sometimes inexpertly corrected by subsequent generations of copyists. There are words that make their only appearance here. Scholarship must guess at their meaning from the context or by analogy with another appearance of the same root in one or another of the related Near Eastern languages. Not infrequently, scholarship sighs and says "Hebrew unclear."

There were choices to be made about the *kind* of English into which we want to translate the Hebrew. We follow the modern trend to avoid the fancy-dress sound of antiquity. We grieve that no twentieth-century English is capable of the thunder at Sinai of the King James Version. The most sophisticated modern scholarship has not produced the old music or the felicitous phrases which so memorably render complex ideas. We console ourselves that new translations don't replace the old, but offer alternatives, correctives, clarifications. King James we will have always with us; what we don't need is Kingjamesese.

We wished to produce an English syntax. There is loss: you can't think Hebrew in English word order. However, if you set down the Hebrew word order, you produce language the Lord never created at Babel: Biblese.

And we chose not to sound solemn. We have known all along that a revisionist piety has overlaid a terrific story with a hush of the sacred. Don't we know our patriarchs and matriarchs grieved, suffered, and sinned like us? Why are we surprised that they laugh as we laugh, and talk colloquially to one another, with their tongues sometimes in their cheeks?

It took me some three years of work to come up with my translation, which I handed to Rabbi Jules Harlow to check word for word with the Hebrew Bible, and he took everything I had done apart again. His heart and his ear kept yearning for the Hebrew, forcing me to keep trying to find English closer to the original. He relayed to me relevant portions of the Hebrew commentaries of Moses Hirsch Segal and Judah Kil. We sat together hour after hour, afternoons on end, adopting the principle of the Targums*— the Aramaic translations of the Hebrew which insisted on understanding and clarifying the obscurities of the difficult text and which were used not instead of, but in addition to, the rigorous and difficult Hebrew. I am grateful for his suggestions and advice; responsibility for the translation that follows is entirely mine.

—Lore Segal
New York, 1991

* See Roger Le Déant in *The Cambridge History of Judaism*, Séminair Français, Rome.

THE STORY OF KING SAUL AND KING DAVID

THERE WAS A MAN FROM RAMAH, a Zuphite from the hill country of Ephraim and his name was Elkanah, son of Jeroham, son of Elihu, son of Tohu, son of Zuph, of the tribe of Ephraim. He had two wives. One was called Hannah and the other Peninnah. Peninnah had borne children, but Hannah had no children. Once a year this man left his town to go up to worship and sacrifice to the Lord of hosts at Shiloh where Eli's two sons, Hophni and Phinehas, were priests of the Lord. Every time Elkanah sacrificed he gave his wife Peninnah and each of her sons and daughters a portion of the meat, but to Hannah he gave only one portion for, although Hannah was the one he loved, the Lord had closed her womb. Her rival was always looking for ways to provoke Hannah and to mortify her because the Lord had closed her womb. So it went year after year. When they came up to the house of the Lord, Peninnah would provoke her and Hannah cried and

wouldn't eat, and her husband, Elkanah, would say, Why do you cry, Hannah, and why won't you eat? Why are you so unhappy? Aren't I worth more to you than ten sons?

Once, at Shiloh, when they had finished eating, Hannah got up and went and stood before the Lord. Now Eli, the priest, was sitting in his seat by the door of the temple of the Lord. Out of her unhappy heart Hannah prayed to the Lord and wept bitterly and vowed a vow and said, Lord of hosts, if You will only see Your maidservant's misery and keep me in Your mind and not forget me and give Your maidservant a man-child, I will give him into Your service. He shall drink no wine or any strong drink; no razor shall touch his head. And as she prayed and kept praying

to the Lord, Eli was watching her mouth, for Hannah was speaking to her heart. Only her lips moved and one couldn't hear her voice. Eli thought she was drunk and said, How long are you going to carry on like this? Sober up! But Hannah answered, No, my lord! I'm a bitterly unhappy woman. I have drunk no wine or any strong drink but am pouring my heart out to the Lord. You mustn't think of your servant as some godless woman! I have been speaking out of the overfullness of my misery and mortification. Eli said, Go in peace, and may the God of Israel give you whatever you have asked Him. She said, Think kindly of your servant! Then the woman went her way and ate and drank and stopped looking so unhappy.

They rose early in the morning, prostrated themselves before the Lord, and returned home to Ramah. And Elkanah lay with his wife Hannah, and the Lord kept her in His mind. Hannah conceived and the year turned and she bore a son and called him Samuel, meaning, I asked the Lord for him. Now when Elkanah and all his household went up to offer the yearly sacrifice and fulfill his vow to the Lord, Hannah did not go with them. She said, When the child is weaned I will bring him into the presence of the Lord, and there he shall remain all the days of his life. Her husband, Elkanah, said, Do whatever you think best. Stay here till you have weaned him, and may the Lord prove the words your mouth has spoken. And so the woman stayed and nursed her son, and when she had weaned him, she took him up to Shiloh with her, and took along a three-year-old bull, a measure of flour, and a jar of wine, and brought him into the house of the Lord, and the boy was just a little boy. They slaughtered the bull and they brought the little boy to Eli. And she said, Ah, my lord, as your soul lives, I'm that woman who stood here beside you and prayed to the Lord, and this is the boy for whom I prayed. The Lord has given me my wish. Now I wish to give him to the Lord for all the days of his life. And they bowed down to the Lord and they left the child there.

▪ ▪

AND Hannah prayed to the Lord and said, My heart is happy in the Lord! The Lord raises my head high! My mouth is stretched wide to mock my enemies. I laugh in the joy of Your salvation.

No one is holy like the Lord; there is no one except You, nor is there any rock like our God!

Stop all this boasting and impertinence! Your mouth spouts too much arrogance, for the Lord is a God who knows everything and weighs every deed.

The bow of the mighty is broken, and those who have stumbled are girded with power.

Those who had plenty hire themselves out for bread, and those who went hungry fatten on food.

The barren woman has borne seven sons, and the mother of many pines.

The Lord puts to death and brings to life. He sends us down to Sheol and brings us back up.

The Lord makes poor and makes rich, throws down and raises up. He raises the poor from the dust, and raises the beggar from the dung hill to seat him in the place of honor among princes, for the foundations of the earth belong to the Lord; upon them He has built the world.

He guides the feet of His faithful while the wicked perish in darkness; it is not man's strength that gives man power.

Those who quarrel with the Lord shall be crushed. He thunders against them in the heavens.

The Lord judges the earth from end to end.

He will give His king power and raise high the head of His anointed!

Then Elkanah and Hannah went home to Ramah and the boy served the Lord under the eye of Eli, the priest.

▪ ▪

Now Eli's sons were impious men, who cared nothing for the Lord nor for what was customary between the people and the priest. When a man offered a sacrifice, the priest's boy used to come while the meat of the burnt offering was cooking, and would stick a three-pronged fork into the kettle, or cauldron, or pan, and whatever the fork happened to bring out, the priest took for himself. That's how it was always done when the children of Israel came to Shiloh. But now the priest's boy would come to the man when he was sacrificing before the fat had so much as burned away and would say, Give me the meat raw. The priest likes his meat roasted, not boiled. If the man said, Just let the fat burn off as always and then you can take as much as you want, the boy would say, No, give it

to me now, or I'll make you! It was a very great sin, for these young men were making a mockery of the Lord's sacrifice right under the Lord's eye.

But Samuel served the Lord as temple boy and wore the linen shirt of a priest of God. Every year his mother made him a little coat and brought it up to Shiloh, when she came with her husband to offer the yearly sacrifice. And Eli the priest blessed Elkanah and his wife and said, May the Lord give you children in return for the boy you have given to the Lord's service. Then they returned home, and the Lord kept Hannah in His mind and she conceived and bore Elkanah three more sons and two daughters. But the boy Samuel grew up in the service of the Lord.

And Eli had grown very old and heard

what his sons were doing to the children of Israel, and how they lay with the women who served at the doors of the tent of the congregation, and he spoke to them and said, Why do you do these wicked things that I hear people saying about you?

Don't, my sons! These are bad reports that I hear spreading among the people of the Lord! If a man sins against another man, God can judge between them, but who is there to intercede for the sinner against God? But the young men would not hear what their father said, for God was determined to destroy them.

And all the while, Samuel was growing up and he pleased God and men.

And a man from God came to Eli and said to him, The Lord has spoken and He says, Didn't I make Myself known to your father's house when Israel was in bondage to the house of Pharaoh in Egypt, and didn't I choose you of all the tribes of Israel to be My priests and serve at My altar and burn incense and to wear the priestly ephod in My presence? To your father's house I assigned Israel's burnt offerings to be your food. Why do you kick at My sacrifices and the offerings which I have commanded in My temple? Do you honor your sons more than Me that you let them fatten on the first portion of all the offerings of My people Israel? Therefore the Lord, the God of Israel, says, Yes, I said that your house and your father's house should walk before me forever, but now, the Lord says, God forbid! It is those who honor Me whom I will honor, but those who throw me off will be thrown off.

Know this: the days are coming when I shall hew off your arm and the arm of your father's house. Never again will there be any old man in your house. You will see your enemy serve in My temple and that everything he does will do Israel good; whereas in your house there shall never be any old man. Nevertheless I will not cut you off altogether from the service at My altar but wear out your eyes in the grief of your soul: most of your house shall die in their manhood.

And it will be a sign to you—what will happen to your two sons, Hophni and Phinehas, who shall die, both on the same day. I shall raise Myself a priest whom I trust to do what is in My heart and in My mind. I will build him a durable house and he will walk before My anointed forever. And it will happen that the remnants of your house will come crawling to him for a penny and a bite of bread, and say, Please, let me serve somewhere in the temple, so that I may have a crust of bread to eat.

▪ ▪

BUT the boy Samuel served the Lord under Eli, in those days when the Lord's word was rare and there were few visions.

It happened one day that Eli was lying in his place, and his eyes had grown so weak that he could not see. The lamp of God was still burning. Samuel lay down in the temple of the Lord where the ark of God was kept. And the Lord called, Samuel! Samuel said, Here I am, and ran to Eli and said, Here I am! You called me. Eli said, No, I didn't. Go and lie down. And he went and lay down. And the Lord called him again, Samuel! He got up and went to Eli and said, Here I am! You called me. But he said, No, my son, I didn't call you. Go and lie down. This was before Samuel knew the Lord, before the word of the Lord had come to him. And the Lord called Samuel a third time, Samuel! And Samuel got up and went to Eli and said, Here I am! You called me! Now Eli understood that the Lord was calling the child and said, Go and lie down, and if you hear the calling again, you must say, Speak, Lord, your servant is listening! And Samuel went back and lay down in his place.

And the Lord came and stood and called as He had done before, Samuel! Samuel! And Samuel said, Speak, Lord, Your servant is listening.

And the Lord said to Samuel, There is something I shall do in Israel that will ring in the two ears of all who shall hear it. On that day I shall bring upon Eli all that I have spoken against his house; what I have begun I shall finish. I have told him that I will judge his house forever because he knew of his sons' sins, and how they mocked Me, and did not prevent them. Therefore they shall die, both on the same day. I have vowed that no offering and no sacrifice shall atone for the guilt of Eli's house.

Samuel lay in his place until morning and he opened the doors of the house of the Lord. And Samuel was afraid to tell Eli his vision. Eli called Samuel and said, Samuel, my son! And he said, Here I am! He said, What did the Lord say to you? Don't you hide anything from me! May God do the same and worse to you if you hide a single word of all that He has said to you! And so Samuel told him everything and hid nothing from him, and Eli

said, He is the Lord and will do whatever He thinks best.

And Samuel grew and the Lord was with him and let no word that Samuel spoke fall to the ground. And all Israel from Dan to Beer-sheba knew that Samuel was the Lord's trusted prophet. And the Lord continued to appear in Shiloh, for the Lord made himself known to Samuel at Shiloh, and Samuel's words spread throughout Israel.

■ ■

AND the time came when the Philistines gathered for battle against Israel, and Israel went to meet them in battle and encamped in Eben-ezer. The Philistines had encamped at Aphek and ranged their forces against Israel. The battle spread, and the Philistines routed Israel and killed some four thousand men on the field of battle.

When the army returned to the camp, the elders of Israel said, Why has the Lord routed us today and handed us over to the Philistines? Let's fetch the ark of the covenant of the Lord from Shiloh. Let it go along with us and deliver us out of the clutches of our enemies. And so the people sent to Shiloh to fetch the ark of the Lord enthroned upon Cherubim, and Eli's two sons, Hophni and Phinehas, came with the ark. When the ark of the Lord arrived in the camp, all the Israelites shouted a great shout that shook the earth. The Philistines heard it and said, What is this great shouting in the Hebrew camp? When the Philistines learned that the ark of the Lord had arrived in the camp, they were frightened and said, the gods have arrived in the camp! What will become of us? Nothing

like this has ever happened before! What will become of us? Who will save us from the hand of these mighty gods? These are the gods who struck Egypt with every kind of plague in the wilderness! Philistines, be strong! Act like men, so you won't become slaves to the very Hebrews who used to be your slaves! Be men, and fight! And so the Philistines fought and routed the Israelites, who fled every man to his own tent. The slaughter was very great. Thirty thousand of Israel's foot soldiers died, and the ark of God was taken, and Eli's two sons, Hophni and Phinehas, died.

And a man of the tribe of Benjamin fled the field of battle and came running to Shiloh that same day with his clothes rent and dust on his head. When he came into the town, Eli was sitting on his seat near the gate, facing up the road, because his heart trembled for the ark of God. The man entered the town and told his news, and the whole town let out a scream. Eli heard the sound of crying and asked, What is this great noise? And the man came running and told Eli the news. Now Eli was eighty-nine years old and could no longer see. The man said, I've come straight from the field and have fled the day's battle. Eli said, And how did it go, my son? The messenger answered, Israel flees before the Philistines, and a great plague has broken out among the people. Your two sons, Hophni and Phinehas, are dead, and the ark of God has been taken. When he spoke of the ark of God, Eli fell backward off his seat and broke his neck and died, for he was an old man and heavy, and had judged in Israel for forty years.

His daughter-in-law, Phinehas's wife, was with child and near her time. When she heard that the ark of God had been taken and that her father-in-law was dead and her husband was dead, she crouched down and gave birth, for her pains began suddenly. As she lay dying, the women who stood around her said, It's all right! You have borne a son! But she did not answer them, or take in what they were saying. She named the boy Ichabod, saying the glory has passed away from Israel because God's ark has been taken, and because of her father-in-law and her husband; therefore she said, The glory has passed away from Israel, for the ark of God has been taken.

· ·

THE Philistines took the ark of God and they brought it from Eben-ezer to Ashdod. And the Philistines took the ark and brought it into the house of the god Dagon and set it up next to Dagon. When the Ashdodites awoke early next morning and came to the house of Dagon, what do you know! There was Dagon, and he had fallen facedown on the ground before the ark of the Lord. So they picked Dagon up and put him back in his place. They woke early next morning, and there he was again— Dagon fallen flat on his face before the ark of the Lord, with his head and both his hands chopped off on the threshold and only the trunk was left in one piece. That is why to this day no priest of Dagon nor anyone who comes into the house of Dagon will step on the threshold of the house of Dagon in Ashdod.

And the hand of the Lord descended upon the Ashdodites. He ravaged them and afflicted them with boils in Ashdod

and in the land round about. When the Ashdodites saw everything that was happening, they said, The ark of the God of Israel can't stay here. His hand weighs down upon us and upon our god Dagon. And they summoned the princes of the Philistines and said, What are we going to do with the ark of the God of Israel? They said, Have the ark of God brought to Gath. And so they brought the ark of God to Gath. No sooner had they brought it to Gath than the hand of God turned against the city and caused a very great terror because He afflicted everyone in the city, young and old, with boils in their secret parts. So they sent the ark of God to Ekron, but when the ark of God came to Ekron, the people of Ekron screamed and said, They've brought the ark of the God of Israel to me here in order to kill me and my kin! And they summoned all the

princes of the Philistines and said, Send the ark of the God of Israel home before it kills me and my kin! And there was a deathly panic in the whole city where the hand of God weighed down upon them, and those who did not die were plagued with boils, and the cry of the city rose to heaven.

• •

THE ark of the Lord was in the land of the Philistines for seven months, and the Philistines summoned the priests and sorcerers and said, What are we going to do with the ark of the Lord? Tell us how to send it home where it belongs! They said, If you want to send the ark of the God of Israel home, don't send it without sending an offering of compensation, and then you will be healed, and you'll find out why His

hand will not let up! They said, What compensation must we pay Him? They answered, Five golden boils, and five golden mice, a number equal to the number of the princes of Philistia, for your princes are struck with the same plague that has stricken you. Make images of your boils and images of your mice that waste your land, and give them in tribute to the God of Israel. Perhaps He will lighten the weight of his hand from you and your gods and your land. Why do you harden your hearts like Pharaoh and the Egyptians? Isn't it true that when He was through playing His games with them, they sent the children of Israel away and they left? Now make a new cart. Take two milch cows that have never been under yoke and harness the cows to the cart, but take their calves that follow behind them, back home. Take the ark of the Lord and lay it

on the cart. Put beside it the pouch with the golden things that you are sending as compensation and let the cart go where it will. Now watch! If it takes the road across the border in the direction of Beth-shemesh, then it was He who brought this great disaster upon us. If not, then we will know it was not His hand that has afflicted us and what happened to us has been a coincidence. So that's what they did. They took two milch cows and harnessed them to the cart, and tied up their calves at home. Then they laid the ark of the Lord on the cart with the pouch of golden mice and the images of their boils. The cows walked straight toward Beth-shemesh, mooing as they went, and kept to the road, turning neither right nor left. And the princes of Philistia followed behind them as far as the border of Beth-shemesh.

The people of Beth-shemesh were har-

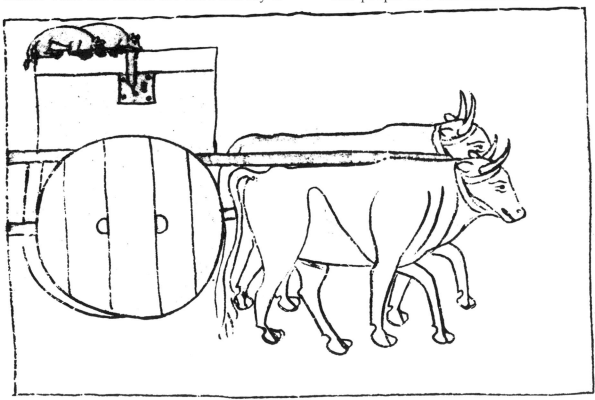

vesting their wheat in the valley and looked up and saw the ark and they rejoiced to see it. When the cart reached the field of Joshua, the Beth-shemeshite, it stopped by a great stone, and they chopped up the wood of the cart and offered the milch cows as a burnt offering to the Lord. The Levites took down the ark of the Lord and the pouches with the golden things and laid them on the great stone. That day the people of Beth-shemesh offered up burnt offerings and sacrificed sacrifices to the Lord, and the five princes of Philistia saw it and returned home that same day to Ekron. And there were five golden boils which the Philistines offered in compensation to the Lord, one for Ashdod, one for Gaza, one for Ashkelon, one for Gath, and one for Ekron. The number of the golden mice was equal to the number of cities belonging to the five Philistine princes, both their fortified cities and unwalled villages. The great stone upon which they laid the ark of the Lord stands in the field of Joshua the Beth-shemeshite to this day.

But the sons of Jeconiah did not rejoice with the people of Beth-shemesh when they saw the ark of the Lord, and He struck down seventy of them.* The people mourned the great number of the people whom the Lord had struck down, and the people of Beth-shemesh said, Who can withstand the presence of the Lord, this holy God? And to whom shall it go to get it away from us? And they sent messengers to the people of Kiriath-jearim and said, The Philistines have returned the ark

---

* Septuagint 6:19.

---

of the Lord. Come down and take it away with you. The men of Kiriath-jearim came and took the ark of God and brought it into the house of Abinadab on the hill, and they consecrated his son Eleazar to take care of the ark of the Lord.

· ·

FOR twenty years from that day the ark stayed in Kiriath-jearim, and the house of Israel returned to the Lord. And Samuel spoke to the house of Israel and said, If you want to return to the Lord with all your heart you must rid yourselves of these alien gods and Astartes. Turn your hearts to the Lord and serve only Him, and He will save you from the Philistines. And the children of Israel rid themselves of the Baals and Astartes and served only the Lord.

And Samuel said, Gather all of Israel at Mizpah and I will pray for you to the Lord. They gathered at Mizpah and drew water and poured it out before the Lord, fasting all day and saying, We have sinned against the Lord. And Samuel judged over the children of Israel at Mizpah.

When the Philistines heard that Israel was gathered at Mizpah, the princes of the Philistines marched against Israel and the children of Israel heard and were afraid of the Philistines and said to Samuel, Don't stop crying to the Lord your God so that He may deliver us out of the hand of the Philistines! Samuel took a suckling lamb and offered it to the Lord whole as a burnt offering and cried to the Lord on behalf of Israel and the Lord answered him. Samuel was offering the burnt offering as the Philistines advanced to battle against Israel, and on that day the Lord thundered against the Philistines with a great voice and threw them into confusion, and the men of Israel routed them and pursued them out of Mizpah and beat them all the way to a point just below Beth-car. And Samuel took a stone and set it up between Mizpah and Jeshanah and called it Ebenezer, meaning stone of our help, and said, This far has the Lord helped us. And so the Philistines were subdued and did not cross the borders of Israel again, for as long as Samuel lived, the Lord kept His hand turned against the Philistines. Israel recovered the cities which the Philistines had taken from Ekron to Gath and the land round about. And there was peace between Israel and the Amorites as well.

As long as Samuel lived, he judged over Israel all the days of his life. Year after year he traveled the circuit from Beth-el to Gilgal and Mizpah, and in all these places he judged over Israel. Then he would return to Ramah, to his own house, and there too he judged Israel, and there he built an altar to the Lord.

▪ ▪

AND Samuel grew old and made his sons judges in Israel. His firstborn son was called Joel, and the name of his second was Abijah. They were judges in Beer-sheba. But his sons did not follow in his footsteps. They went out for profit, took bribes, and bent justice to their own advantage. And the elders of Israel assembled and came to Samuel at Ramah, and said, Look, you

have grown old, and your sons have not followed in your footsteps. Give us a king to judge over us. All the other nations have one! It seemed wrong to Samuel that they were saying, Give us a king to rule over us! Samuel prayed to the Lord. The Lord said, Listen to the people and everything they say to you. It is not you they have discarded; it's Me whom they discard as their king over them. They do to you what they have always done from the day I brought them out of Egypt to this very day—they abandon Me and serve other gods! Listen and do what they say, only warn them of the sort of justice with which this king will rule them.

Samuel told the people, who asked him for a king, every word that the Lord had spoken, and said, This will be the sort of justice with which this king of yours will rule over you: He will take your sons to be his charioteers and horsemen, and outrunners to run in front of his chariots, and to be captains over thousands and over fifties, to plow his fields and reap his harvests, to forge his weapons and build his chariots. He will take your daughters to make his perfumes, and cook for him, and bake for him. He will take the best of your fields and your vineyards and your olive groves, and give them to his servants. What's more, he will seize every tenth part of your fields and your vineyards to give to his eunuchs. He will take your menservants and your maidservants, and the best of your cattle, and your asses and put them to work for him. He will take a tenth part of your flocks, and you yourselves will become his servants. The day shall come when you will cry out loud to Me because of your king whom you have

chosen yourselves, and that will be the day when the Lord will not answer you. But the people refused to hear Samuel's words. They said, No, but let us have a king over us, and then we will be like all the nations, and our king will judge us and lead us and fight our wars!

Samuel heard everything the people said and told it in the Lord's ear, and the Lord said, Listen to what they say. Make them a king to be their king. And Samuel said to the men of Israel, Go home, every man to his city.

▪ ▪

THERE lived in Gibeah a man of the tribe of Benjamin, whose name was Kish, son of Abiel, son of Zeror, son of Becorath, son of Aphiah, a Benjaminite and a man of substance. He had a son named Saul, a young, handsome man. There was no one among the children of Israel handsomer than he and from the shoulder up a head taller than all the people. Now some asses belonging to Saul's father Kish were lost, and Kish said to Saul, Take one of the servants and go and look for the asses!

They went into the hills of Ephraim and through the land of Shalishah and they did not find them; they went through the land of Shaalim, and they were not there. They went all through the lands of Benjamin, but they did not find them. When they came to the land of Zuph, Saul said, Come, let's go home or my father will start worrying about us instead of the asses. But the servant said, Look, there's a man of God who lives in this town, very much respected; whatever he says comes true. Let's go to him. Perhaps he will tell us the way for us to go. Saul said, Yes, but if we go to the man, what can we bring him? We've eaten all the bread in our bags and have none left to bring the man of God for a present. What else do we have? Again the servant answered and said, Look, I've found this quarter-piece of silver. Let me give it to the man of God to tell us our way. Saul said, Well said! Come, let's go. They came to the town where the man of God lived, and as they walked up the slope toward town, they met some girls coming out to draw water, and they asked them, Is the seer here?—For in the old days someone in Israel wanting to go up and ask God a question would say, Come, let's go to the seer. For today's prophets used to be called seers.—The girls answered, Yes! He was just here ahead of you. Hurry up! He's come to town today because the people are going up the hill to sacrifice in the holy place. When you get to town, you'll find him before he goes up to the holy place to eat. The people won't eat till he comes and blesses the sacrifice; then the guests eat. If you go up right away you'll find him.

They went up to the town and were going in the gate, and look, here came Samuel toward them on his way up to the holy place. Now the day before, the Lord had spoken in Samuel's ear and said, To-morrow, about this time, I will send you a man from the land of Benjamin and you will anoint him to be prince over My people Israel, so that he may save My people from the hand of the Philistines for I have seen My people's misery and their crying has reached My ears. Now when Samuel saw Saul, the Lord said, Look, there's the man of whom I said that he would rule over My people. And Saul came toward Samuel inside the gates of the town and said, Can you please tell me which is the house of the seer? Samuel answered, I am the seer. Go up to the holy place ahead of me. Today you will eat with me, and in the morning I'll send you on your way after I have told you everything that is on your mind. As for your asses that have been lost these three days, don't give them a thought. They've been found. What treasure is there in Israel that does not belong to you and your father's house? Saul answered, But I'm only a Benjaminite from the smallest of the tribes of Israel, and my family is the least of the families of the tribes of Benjamin. Why do you say these things to me?

And Samuel took Saul and his servant and brought them into the chamber and seated them at the head of the guests— some thirty men—and Samuel said to the cook, Bring the portion I gave you to put aside! The cook picked up the thigh and the fat tail and set them before Saul, and Samuel said, Look, eat these remains of the sacrifice that is set before you. When I invited these people, it was put aside for you in readiness for this hour. And on that day Saul ate with Samuel. Then they came down the hill into the town and he made a bed for Saul on the roof of the house and Saul lay down and slept. When the sun rose, Samuel called up to the roof to Saul and said, Come, get up, and I'll send you on your way. Saul got up and the two went out together—he and Samuel. And when they came to the end of the town, Samuel said, Tell the servant to walk on ahead of us. The servant walked on ahead, and Samuel said, You stand still so that I

can make the word of God known to you.

And Samuel took a flask of oil and poured it on Saul's head, and kissed him, and said, Know that the Lord has anointed you ruler over His people Israel. When you leave me today, you'll come to the tomb of Rachel on the border of Benjamin at Zelzah, and meet two men, who will say, The asses you went to search for have been found. Look, your father has forgotten all about the asses and is worried about you. He says, What shall I do about my son? You'll walk on and come to the oak of Tabor. There you will meet three men on a pilgrimage to God at Beth-el. One will carry three young goats, one will carry three loaves of bread, and one will carry a jug of wine. They'll give you a friendly greeting and offer you two loaves, and you must take them. After that you'll get to the hill of God, where there is a Philistine garrison, and you will meet a company of prophets walking down from the holy place with lyres and timbrels and flutes going in front of them. They will be in ecstasy. The spirit of the Lord will overcome you and you will be in ecstasy with them and will be changed into another man. And as these signs are mani-

fested to you, do whatever comes to hand, for God is with you. And you will go down to Gilgal ahead of me and look! I'll come down to you to offer burnt offerings and a peace offering. You shall wait seven days until I come to you and tell you what you must do.

And as Saul turned to leave Samuel, God changed his heart into another heart, and all these signs were manifested on that same day. When they came to Gibeah, look! here was a company of prophets walking toward him, and the spirit of God came upon Saul and he became one with them in their ecstasy. All the people who had known him before and saw him speaking in ecstasy with the prophets said one to another, What's happened to Kish's son? Is Saul one of the prophets too? And one of them said, And who is their father? From which comes the saying, Is Saul one of the prophets too?

And when he ceased speaking in ecstasy, Saul came up to the holy place. And Saul's uncle asked him and his servant, Where have you been? Saul said, To look for the asses, and when we couldn't find them anywhere, we went to Samuel. Saul's uncle said, Tell me what Samuel said to you. Saul said, He told us the asses had been found. But he did not tell his uncle what Samuel had said about the kingship.

■ ■

AND Samuel called the people together before the Lord in Mizpah, and he spoke to the children of Israel and said, Hear the word of the Lord! The God of Israel says, It is I who brought Israel out of Egypt and saved you from the hand of the Egyptians and from the hand of all the kingdoms that have oppressed you. Today you have thrown off your God, who saved you in your greatest need and distress. You said, No, but put a king over us! Well, then, approach the Lord according to your tribes and your thousands.

Now Samuel let all the tribes of Israel approach before the Lord and the lot fell upon the tribe of Benjamin. When Samuel let the tribe of Benjamin approach before the Lord, the lot fell upon the clan of Matri, and when he let the clan of Matri approach man by man, the lot fell upon Saul son of Kish. And they looked for him, but he was nowhere to be found. And they approached the Lord again and asked Him, Is it perhaps that he hasn't come here? But the Lord said, Look among the baggage. He is hiding. And so they ran over and brought him out, and he stood amongst the people and was taller by a head than all the people. Then Samuel spoke to the people and said, Look! This is he whom the Lord has chosen, for there is no one like him among all this people! And the people shouted for joy and said, Long live the king! Then Samuel told the people the law of the kingdom and wrote it in the book and laid it before the Lord, and Samuel let the people go, each man to his own house.

And Saul too went home to Gibeah, and with him went those of the soldiers whose hearts God had touched. But there were

some—a godless lot—who said, And this is the fellow who's going to save us from the Philistines? And they laughed at him and brought no presents, but Saul acted as if he hadn't heard.

■ ■

AND Nahash, king of the Ammonites, marched against Israel and laid siege to the city of Jabesh-gilead, and the people of Jabesh said to Nahash, Make a covenant with us and we will be your servants.

Nahash said, The covenant that I will make with you will be to gouge out everyone's right eye and put the whole of Israel to shame. The elders of Jabesh said, Give us seven days so we can send messengers throughout Israel. If no one saves us, we will come out and surrender to you.

When the messengers came to Saul's Gibeah and told the news, the people wept aloud. And, look, here came Saul from the field walking behind the oxen. He said, What has happened to make the people cry? They told him the news from Jabesh. When he heard what they were saying, the spirit of God came upon Saul. He burned with rage and took a yoke of oxen and hewed them into pieces which he sent by messenger throughout the land of Israel, saying, This is what's going to be done to the cattle of anyone who does not follow Saul and Samuel into battle.

And the Lord's terror came upon the people and they set out as one man. He mustered them in Bezek and there were three hundred thousand of the children of Israel and thirty thousand men from Judah. To the messenger from Jabesh he said, This is what you shall say to the men of Jabesh-gilead: Tomorrow when the sun is high, you'll be rescued. When the messengers came home and told the men of Jabesh, they were glad and sent word to the Ammonites and said, Tomorrow we'll come out and surrender to you. Do with us whatever you like.

And so it happened next morning. Saul divided the soldiers into three columns and entered the camp at the morning watch and battered the Ammonites till the sun was high, and those who were left over scattered so that no two of them remained together. And the people said to Samuel, Where are those louts who said, Is this the fellow who is going to save us from the Philistines? Hand them over so we can kill them! But Saul said, There'll be no killing on this day when the Lord has given Israel a victory! And Samuel spoke to the people and said, Come, let us go to Gilgal and there we will celebrate the kingship anew. And all the people came to Gilgal, where they made Saul king before the Lord in Gilgal and offered a peace offering to the Lord, and Saul and all the men of Israel were very glad.

■ ■

AND Samuel spoke to all of Israel and said, Look, I listened to everything you said to me and have given you a king to rule over you. Look, now you have a king to lead you, and I have grown old and gray and look, my sons live among you. It is I who have led you from my youth until this day. Here I stand. Accuse me to the Lord and to His anointed. Whose ox or ass have

I taken? Whom have I ever wronged or abused? At whose hand have I received a bribe to blind my eyes? I will give it back! They said, You have never wronged or abused us. You never took anything from anyone. He said to them, The Lord and His anointed are your witnesses this day that you have found nothing in my hands. They said, Yes, they are witnesses.

And Samuel said, It is the Lord who appointed Moses and Aaron and brought your fathers up out of the land of Egypt. Now stand and be judged in the presence of the Lord's beneficence to you and to your fathers, which I shall recount to you. After Jacob came to Egypt and your fathers cried to the Lord, the Lord sent Moses and Aaron to lead your fathers out of Egypt to live in this land. But when they forgot the Lord their God, He sold them into the hand of Sisera, the commander of the army of Hazor, and into the hand of the Philistines, and into the hand of the king of Moab, and they made war against them. They cried to the Lord and said, We have sinned, for we turned away from the Lord to serve Baals and Astartes! Only save us from the hand of our enemies and we will serve you! So the Lord sent Jerubbaal, and Bedan, and Jephthah, and Samson and saved you from the hand of the enemies that surrounded you, and you lived in safety. But when you saw Nahash, the king of the Ammonites, marching against you, you said to me, No, but we want a king to rule over us—even though the Lord your God is your King! Well, here is the king for whom you have asked. The Lord has given you a king to rule over you. If you fear the Lord and serve Him and listen to His voice and don't rebel against the words of the Lord's mouth, then the king who rules over you will follow the Lord your God. But if you don't listen to the voice of the Lord and rebel against the words of His mouth, His hand will be against you as it was against your fathers.

Therefore stand before me and you will see a great thing that the Lord is going to do right before your eyes. Isn't this the dry time of the wheat harvest? I will call upon the Lord, and He will make it thunder and rain so that you will see and understand your wickedness in the Lord's eyes, when you asked for a king. And Samuel called upon the Lord and the Lord made it thunder and rain, and that day the people were very much afraid of the Lord and of Samuel. And the people said, Pray to the Lord your God so your servants will not die because on top of all our sins we have asked for a king! Then Samuel said, Don't be afraid! You have acted wickedly but don't turn from the Lord. Serve Him with your whole heart. Don't follow after these nothings! Idols are useless and can't save you, because they're nothing. The Lord will not abandon His people for His great Name's sake, for the Lord was pleased to make you a people for Himself. As for me, God forbid that I should sin against the Lord by ceasing to pray for you and to teach you the good and right way. Only fear the Lord and serve Him truly, and with all your heart for the great things that He has done for you, but if you act wickedly, you and your king will be lost.

▪ ▪

AND Saul became king and reigned over Israel and had reigned two years when he picked himself an army of three thousand men of Israel. Two thousand were under his command in Michmas and in the hill country of Beth-el, and one thousand were with Jonathan at Gibeah in Benjamin. The rest of the army he sent home, each man to his own tent.

And Jonathan killed the Philistine guard at Gibeah. When the Philistines heard, they said, The Hebrews are in revolt! But Saul sounded the ram's horn throughout the land of Israel. And all Israel heard that Saul had killed the Philistine guard, and that Israel was in bad odor with the Philistines, and they rallied to Saul in Gilgal. And the Philistines gathered their forces against Israel—thirty thousand chariots and six thousand horsemen, and the number of their foot soldiers was like the grains of sand on the shores of the sea, and they encamped at Michmas, east of Beth-aven. The men of Israel saw that they were hard-pressed and in great danger, and the people ran and hid in caves and thickets, and in the cleft of the rocks, and trenches, and pits, and some crossed over Jordan into the land of Gad and Gilead.

But Saul stayed in Gilgal, and the people who followed him shook with fright. And Saul waited the seven days Samuel had appointed, but he did not come to Gilgal, and Saul's men were beginning to run away. And Saul said, Bring me the animals for the burnt offering and the peace offering, and he offered the burnt offering. And it happened as he finished offering up the burnt offering, look! here came Samuel! Saul went forward to meet and to

greet him, but Samuel said, What have you done?

Saul said, It's because I saw the people beginning to run away, and you didn't come on the appointed day, and the Philistines were gathering at Michmas! I said to myself, The Philistines will come down upon me at Gilgal before I have prayed to the Lord, and so I made myself offer up the burnt offering! Samuel said, You've acted the fool! Had you obeyed the command that the Lord your God commanded you, He would have established your kingship in Israel forever, but now your kingship will not endure. The Lord has found Himself a man after His own heart to be prince over His people, because you did not obey the Lord's command.

Then Samuel left Gilgal and went his way, and what was left of the army followed Saul from Gilgal to Gibeah in the land of Benjamin, and Saul mustered the soldiers he had with him and there were some six hundred men. And Saul and his son Jonathan and their soldiers stayed at Gibeah in Benjamin.

The Philistines were encamped in Michmas and sent out their raiders in three squadrons. One took the Ophrah Road toward the land of Shual, another took the Geba Road, and yet another the border road that overlooks the Valley of the Hyenas.

And there was no smith to be found in all the land of Israel, because the Philistines said, What if the Hebrews make themselves iron swords and spears? Everyone in Israel had to go down to the Philistines to sharpen his plow or his mattock or his axe or his sickle, and pay them a pim or a third of a shekel to sharpen a plow or a pick or an axe or an ox-goad. When the time came to go into battle, there was not one sword or spear to be found in the hand of any of Saul's or Jonathan's soldiers. Only Saul and Jonathan bore weapons.

Now a Philistine outpost had advanced into the narrow pass of Michmas. It happened one day that Jonathan son of Saul said to his young arms-bearer, Come, let's cross over to the Philistine outpost! And he did not tell his father. Saul was still in the outskirts of Gibeah, sitting under the pomegranate at Migron. There were with him some six hundred men, and Ahijah son of Ahitub, the brother of Ichabod son of Phinehas son of Eli, who had been the priest of the Lord at Shiloh, wore his priestly ephod. And nobody knew that Jonathan was gone.

Now there was a jagged rock on one side of the pass through which Jonathan wanted to cross to the Philistine outpost, and a jagged rock on the other. One was called Bozez and the other Seneh. One stood on the north facing Michmas and the other on the south facing Geba. And Jonathan said to the arms-bearer, Come, let's cross over to the outpost of these uncircumcised louts. Perhaps the Lord will help us. There's nothing to prevent the Lord from winning a victory whether it's with many or with a few! His arms-bearer said, Do whatever your heart tells you to do. I'm with you! Jonathan said, We'll cross where the men will see us. If they say, Stay where you are, we're coming down! then we will stay where we are and we won't go up. But if they say, Come up

here! it will be our sign that the Lord has delivered them into our hands. So the two of them crossed where the Philistine outpost could see them. The Philistines said, Look at that! The Hebrews are coming out of the holes where they've been hiding themselves! And the men of the outpost called to Jonathan and his arms-bearer and said, Come up here and we'll show you a thing or two! And Jonathan said to his arms-bearer, Follow me! The Lord has delivered them into Israel's hands! Jonathan climbed up on his hands and knees with his arms-bearer coming behind him, and they fell before Jonathan, and his arms-bearer kept behind him and finished them off. And it happened at the first strike that Jonathan and his arms-bearer killed some twenty men in a field no bigger than a yoke of oxen is able to plow in a day.

And a horror came upon the Philistines inside the camp and out in the field, and the soldiers, and the outpost, and the raiders were frightened, and the earth shuddered with the horror of God. Saul's watchmen at Gibeah in Benjamin saw the commotion of the multitude wavering this way and that. And Saul told his soldiers to call the roll and see who was missing, and they called the roll and what do you know! Jonathan and his arms-bearer were gone! Saul called Ahijah and said, Bring me the ephod—for in those days Ahijah wore the priestly robe in Israel—but even as Saul spoke with the priest, the commotion inside the Philistine camp kept growing and Saul said to the priest, Put your hands down. And Saul and all his soldiers gathered and went into battle, and look! the Philistines in their very great confusion turned their swords against one another. As for the Hebrews who had gone over to the Philistines and had gone into battle with them, they too joined the Israelites who fought with Saul and Jonathan. And all those Israelites who had hidden themselves in the hills of Ephraim heard that the Philistines were in flight, and they too joined the battle and gave chase. And the Lord gave Israel a victory that day and the fighting spread all the way to Beth-aven.

The whole army—some ten thousand men—was with Saul and the battle spread through the city and into the hills of Ephraim, and Saul made a vow on that day and said, A curse upon the man who eats before night falls and I have avenged myself upon my enemies! And all that day no one ate anything. And the men came to a forest and there was a honeycomb. The honey was spilled onto the ground, but not a one put his hand to his mouth, for the soldiers feared the oath. Only Jonathan, who had not heard his father swear this oath, reached down the tip of the staff he carried in his hand and dipped it in the honey, and when he brought it to his mouth, his eyes brightened. One of the soldiers said, Your father has sworn an oath and said, A curse upon the man who eats any food today, and the army is very tired. Jonathan said, My father has made trouble for the people. Look how my eyes have brightened because I tasted a little bit of honey. If the soldiers had eaten the spoils they took from their enemy, we could have struck a greater blow against the Philistines.

And they defeated the Philistines from Michmas to Aijalon, and the army was tired out and fell upon the spoil and took sheep and cattle and calves and slaughtered them there, on the ground, and ate the meat with its blood. They told Saul, Look how the soldiers sin against the Lord! They eat the meat with the blood. He said, You sin against the Lord! Roll that big stone over here. And Saul said, Walk among the soldiers and say, Let each man bring me his ox or his sheep and slaughter it and eat it here so you will not sin against the Lord by eating the meat with the blood. And the soldiers brought him everything—whatever each one had—and there they slaughtered it. And Saul built the Lord an altar, and it was the first altar that Saul built to the Lord.

Saul said, Let's go after the Philistines tonight. We'll plunder them until daybreak and leave them not a man alive! They said, Do whatever you think best! But the priest said, Let's go up and ask God! And Saul went up and asked God, Shall I go down against the Philistines? Will You deliver them into Israel's hand? But that day the Lord did not answer him. Saul called his commanders and said, Go and find out what it is of which we're guilty this day, and by the life of the Lord, who gives the victory to Israel, if it were the fault of my son Jonathan, he should be put to death. And not a man among them answered him. To the Israelites he said, Stand on one side. Jonathan and I will stand on the other. And the whole army said, Do whatever you think best.

Saul said, O Lord, God of Israel! Why have You not answered Your servant this day? If the sin is mine, or my son Jonathan's, then Lord, God of Israel, let the Urim condemn us. But if it's the fault of Your people Israel, let the Thummim acquit us. The lot was cast and it fell upon Saul and Jonathan and cleared the people. Saul said, Cast the lot between me and my son Jonathan, and let the Lord show which must die. And the lot was cast between him and his son Jonathan, and it fell upon Jonathan. And Saul asked Jonathan, Tell me what you have done! Jonathan said, I tasted a little honey on the tip of the staff I carried in my hand, and now I must die! Saul said, May God do the same to me and worse, Jonathan, you must die. But the army said, Shall Jonathan, who has brought Israel this great victory, die? As God lives, not a hair of his head shall fall to the ground, for God was with him in what he did today. And so the army saved Jonathan from death.

After this Saul stopped pursuing the Philistines, and the Philistines returned home. And Saul confirmed his kingship over Israel and fought all his enemies on all sides—Moab and the Ammonites, Edom, and the kings of Zobah, and the Philistines, and wherever he turned he wreaked havoc. He defeated Amalek and rescued Israel out of the hands of the plunderers.

∙ ∙

Now Saul's sons were Jonathan, Ishvi, and Malchi-shua. He had two daughters and the name of the firstborn was Merab, and the name of the younger was Michal. Saul's wife was named Ahinoam, the daughter of Ahimaaz. The commander of

Saul's army was called Abner, the son of Saul's uncle, Ner. Saul's father Kish and Abner's father Ner were the sons of Abiel. The war against the Philistines was bitter for as long as Saul lived, and whenever he saw a powerful and stalwart man, he recruited him into his army.

∙ ∙

SAMUEL said, The Lord sent me to anoint you king over His people Israel. Now hear the word of the Lord! The Lord of hosts has spoken and He says, I remember Amalek and what he did to Israel, and how he lay in wait when Israel came up from Egypt. Go and kill Amalek! Execute the sacred massacre upon all that is his. Have no pity. Kill man and woman, the weaned child and the baby at the breast, the ox

and the sheep and the camel and the ass. And Saul called out the soldiers and mustered them in Telaim—two hundred thousand foot soldiers and ten thousand men from Judah. And Saul came to the city of the Amalekites and lay in wait in the valley. He sent word to the Kenites and said, Go! Leave, and move away from the Amalekites so I don't wipe you out together with them. You treated the children of Israel kindly when they came up from Egypt. And the Kenites moved away from the Amalekites.

And Saul routed the Amalekites from Havilah to Shur on the borders of Egypt. He took Agag, the king of Amalek, alive, but upon the people he executed the sacred massacre with the edge of the sword. And Saul and the soldiers spared Agag and what was best of the flocks and herds, for they did not want to execute the sacred massacre upon the fat animals and young lambs; everything useless and without value, that they massacred. Now the word of the Lord came to Samuel saying, I am sorry that I made Saul king. He has turned against Me and has not carried out My commands. Samuel was angry. All night he cried out loud to the Lord.

Early next morning Samuel rose and went to meet Saul. They told him that Saul had come to Carmel and look! he'd erected himself a monument of victory and moved on and had gone down to Gilgal. Now when Samuel met Saul, Saul said, The Lord's blessing upon you, Samuel, I have carried out the Lord's command. Samuel said, Then what's this bleating of sheep in my ears and why do I hear the lowing of cattle? Saul said, They've been brought up from Amalek. The people spared the best of the flocks and herds to sacrifice to the Lord your God. The rest we massacred for the Lord. Samuel said, Stop it! I'm going to tell you what the Lord told me last night. And Saul said, Tell me. Samuel said, Don't you remember how small you were in your own eyes, and now you are the head of the tribes of Israel? The Lord anointed you king over Israel. Now the Lord sent you to do something. He said, Massacre the sinners—these Amalekites! Fight till you have destroyed them. Why didn't you do what the Lord said? You grabbed the spoil and kept it for yourself in defiance of the Lord's will. Saul said, But I've done what the Lord said! I went when He sent me and brought Agag, king of the Amalekites here, and executed the sacred massacre upon all the Amalekites. It's the people who took some of the oxen and the sheep from the spoils—the best of what was set aside for the sacred massacre, in order to sacrifice it to the Lord your God at Gilgal.

Samuel said, And do burnt offerings and sacrifices please the Lord as much as obedience to His word? To listen is better than to sacrifice, and to hear better than the fat of rams. Disobedience is as sinful as sorcery, and rebelliousness as wicked as idolatry. Because you have turned against the Lord's word, He has turned against you. You are not going to be king.

Saul said, I have sinned. I did not do what the Lord commanded. I was afraid and listened to the voice of the people and not the voice of the Lord. Forgive me my sin, and go back with me so that I may worship the Lord! But Samuel said, I won't go back with you because you have turned against the Lord's word and you will not be king of Israel! Samuel turned to go, but Saul caught the corner of Samuel's coat, and it tore off. Samuel said, Today God has torn the kingdom of Israel out of your hand to give to another who is better than you.

The Everlasting of Israel does not lie and does not change His mind, because He is not a man, who changes His mind. Saul said, I have sinned, but honor me, I beg you, here, in front of the elders and all of Israel. Go back with me so that I may pray to the Lord your God! And so Samuel went back with him and Saul bowed down to the Lord, and Samuel said, Bring me Agag, king of Amalek! And Agag came and stood before him in chains and said, I have left bitterness of death behind me! Samuel said, Your sword has made women childless, and your mother shall be another such childless woman! And Samuel hewed Agag to pieces in the presence of the Lord in Gilgal. Then Samuel returned to Ramah, and Saul went up to Gibeah.

··

SAMUEL never saw Saul again to the day he died, and yet he grieved over Saul, because the Lord was sorry that He had made Saul king of Israel.

··

AND the Lord said, How long will you grieve over Saul, when I have thrown him off? I will not have him king of Israel! Fill your horn with oil and go. I will send you to Jesse the Beth-lehemite. I have found Myself a king from among his sons. Samuel said, How can I go? Saul will hear about it and kill me! But the Lord said, Take a young cow with you and say, I have come to sacrifice to the Lord. Invite Jesse to the sacrifice. I will let you know what you must do to anoint Me the one I tell you.

Samuel did as the Lord said and went to Beth-lehem, and the elders of the town came to meet him trembling and saying, Do you come in peace? Samuel said, Yes. I come in peace to sacrifice to the Lord. Purify yourselves and come and sacrifice with me today.

And he sent to Jesse and his sons to tell them to purify themselves and invited them to the sacrifice. When they came and Samuel saw Jesse's son Eliab, he said to himself, There stands the Lord's anointed! But the Lord said, Don't look at his good looks or his fine figure; I have rejected him. God does not see as man sees. Man sees what is before his eyes, but the Lord sees into the heart. And Jesse had Abinadab pass in front of Samuel, but Samuel said, This is not the one whom the Lord has chosen. Jesse had Shammah pass in front of Samuel, but he said, This is not the one whom the Lord has chosen either. Jesse had his seven sons pass in front of Samuel, but he said, The Lord has chosen none of them.

And Samuel said, Don't you have any other young men? He said, The only one left is the youngest, but look, he's a shepherd, out with the sheep. Samuel said, Send for him. We won't sit down to eat till he comes. Jesse sent to fetch him and he came, rosy-cheeked, with beautiful eyes, and handsome. The Lord said to Samuel, Go and anoint him! He is the one! And Samuel took the horn of oil and anointed him in the presence of all his brothers, and the spirit of the Lord came upon David and was with him from that day on, and Samuel got up and went home to Ramah.

And the spirit of the Lord left Saul, and the Lord's evil spirit made him afraid. The men of Saul's court said, Look, the Lord's evil spirit makes you feel afraid. Only let our lord command his servants to look for a man who knows how to play the lyre. When the Lord's evil spirit troubles you, his hand will play and you will feel better. Saul said, Only find me such a man who knows how to play the lyre, and bring him to me! One of his young men spoke up and said, Look, I hear that Jesse the Beth-lehemite has a son who knows how to play, a brave man and a good fighter, who speaks well and is handsome, and the Lord is with him. Saul sent his messengers to Jesse to say, Send me your son David, the one who tends the flocks! Jesse took an ass, loaded it with loaves of bread, a skin of wine, and a young goat, and sent his son David to bring it to Saul.

And so David came to Saul and served Saul, and Saul came to love David and made him his arms-bearer. Saul sent word to Jesse to say, Let me keep David in my service; I am pleased with him. And whenever the Lord's evil spirit made Saul feel afraid, David took up his lyre and played, and Saul was comforted, and felt better and the evil spirit left him.

∙∙

AND the Philistines called up their forces to battle and gathered at Socoh in Judah, and encamped between Socoh and Azekah in Ephes-dammim. Saul and the men of Israel gathered and encamped in the Valley of Elah and deployed themselves for battle against the Philistines. The Philistines stood on a hill on one side, and Israel stood on a hill on the other side, with the valley between them. And there stepped forward out of the ranks of the Philistines the giant Goliath of Gath, six cubits plus one hand high with a bronze helmet on his head, dressed in plate armor that weighed five thousand bronze shekels. He had bronze greaves upon his legs and a bronze javelin the size of a weaver's beam across his shoulders. The blade weighed six hundred iron shekels, and his shield-bearer walked in front of him. He stood and shouted at the armies of Israel and said, You have come out to fight, have you! So! I'm a Philistine, aren't I? And aren't you Saul's slaves? Choose yourselves one man and send him down to me! If he fights with me and kills me, we will be your slaves, but if I win and kill him, then you shall be our slaves and serve us! The Philistine said, Today I have made a mockery of the army of Israel. I said, Send me a man and we will fight together! When Saul and the children of Israel heard what the Philistine said, they were scared and mortified.

Now David was the son of a certain man of Ephrat, a Beth-lehemite from Judah, who was called Jesse and had eight sons. In the days of Saul, Jesse was getting on in years—an old man, advanced in years, but his three eldest sons followed Saul into battle. Their names were Eliab, the first-born, Abinadab the second, and Shammah the third. David was the youngest. While the three eldest followed Saul to the wars, David, the young one, left Saul's service and returned home to tend his father's sheep in Beth-lehem.

Morning and evening, for forty days, the Philistine came out and stood and mocked the armies of Israel. Now Jesse called his son David and said, Go and take your brothers some roasted corn and these ten loaves of bread. Hurry to the camp and give this to your brothers. These ten fresh cheeses take to the commander of a thousand, and see if your brothers are well and bring me back news of them. They are with Saul and the soldiers of Israel in the valley of Elah fighting the Philistines. David set out early in the morning. He left a man to guard his flock and took the provisions as his father had commanded him and found the camp. The army was already afoot and getting ready for battle. David heard the war cries of Israel and the Philistines deployed for battle, army against army. David left the provisions under guard and ran and found his brothers in the ranks and asked them how they were doing, and as he stood talking with them, look, the giant Goliath came stepping out of the ranks of the Philistines and made his speech. David listened, but all the soldiers of Israel who saw the man got very scared and ran away, saying, Did you see him? He comes out to laugh at Israel! If we had a man who could kill him, the king would make him very rich! He'd give him his own daughter in marriage! His father's house would never pay another tax in Israel! David talked with the men who stood around him and said, Is that what you think they'd do for the man who killed that Philistine and put an end to Israel's shame? Who is that uncircumcised Philistine to mock the armies of the living God? And again the soldiers said, This, that, and the other is what the king would do for any man who killed him. Eliab, David's eldest brother, heard him talking with the soldiers and got angry at David and said, What did you come here for? Who's looking after our few poor sheep in the wilderness? You've got your nerve! Don't think that I don't know your impudence! Coming out here just to watch

the fighting! But David said, What did I do now? I was only asking! And he turned away and asked another soldier the same question and all the soldiers gave him the same answer.

The men heard David talking and told Saul, and he sent for him. David said to Saul, Why should one be afraid of the fellow? Let your servant go fight with that Philistine! But he said, You can't go and fight the Philistine; you're only a boy and he's been a warrior since his boyhood. David said, Your servant has been tending his father's sheep, and when a lion or a

bear came and carried off a lamb of the flock, I would chase it and fight with it, and snatch the lamb out of its mouth. And if it turned on me, I caught it by the throat, wrestled it to the ground, and killed it. Your servant has slain lions and bears and I'll do the same to the uncircumcised Philistine, for he has mocked the armies of the living God. And he said, The Lord who saved me from the lion and the bear will save me from that Philistine! Saul said, Well, then go, and may the Lord be with you! And Saul armed David with his own armor, and put a bronze helmet on his head, and a coat of mail, and David girded Saul's sword over the armor and tried to walk and couldn't, because he'd never done it before. And David said, I can't walk with these things on, because I'm not used to it, and he took them off and took his stick in his hand, chose five smooth stones out of the brook and put them in his shepherd's bag that served him for a pouch, took his sling in his hand, and went to meet the Philistine.

The Philistine came toward David with his shield-bearer walking in front of him. When the Philistine looked up and saw David, he laughed because he was so young and rosy-cheeked and handsome. The Philistine said, What am I, a dog that you come after me with sticks? And he cursed David in the name of his gods, and said, Come here! I'm going to feed your flesh to the birds in the sky and the beasts of the field! David said, You come

against me with sword and spear and javelin, but I come against you in the name of the Lord of hosts, the God of the armies of Israel, whom you have mocked. This day will the Lord deliver you into my hands and I will kill you and cut off your head and serve your carcass and the carcasses of the Philistine camp to the birds in the sky and the beasts of the field. The whole earth will know there is a God in Israel, and all this assembly will know the Lord saves without sword or spear. His is the battle and He has given you into our hands. The Philistine came striding toward David, and David ran and raced toward him, put his hand into his shepherd's bag, took out a stone and slung it, and struck the Philistine in the forehead, and drove the stone into his forehead so that he fell facedown on the ground. That's how David overcame Goliath with sling and stone and struck him down and killed him, and there was no sword in David's hand. And David ran and stood over

the Philistine, drew the sword out of its sheath and finished him off and cut off his head.

When the Philistines saw their champion was dead, they fled, and the men of Israel and Judah rose with a shout of war and chased them all the way to Gath and to the gates of Ekron, and the Philistines fell dead on the road to Shaaraim all the way to Gath and to Ekron. When the children of Israel returned from pursuing the Philistines, they plundered the Philistine camp. But David took that Philistine's head and brought it to Jerusalem. The Philistine's weapons he put in the tent of the Lord.

Now King Saul had watched David going to meet the Philistine and asked Abner, the commander of the army, Whose son is that boy? Abner said, For the life of me, my lord king, I have no idea. The king said, Go and find out whose son this young fellow is. And so when David came back from killing the Philistine, Abner

took him and brought him to Saul and he had the Philistine's head in his hand. Saul said, Whose son are you, my boy? David said, Your servant is the son of Jesse the Beth-lehemite.

■ ■

By the time David and Saul finished speaking, Jonathan's soul had twined itself with David's soul and he loved David as he loved himself. From that day on, Saul kept David with him and did not let him go home to his father's house. And Jonathan struck a covenant with David, because he loved him as he loved his own soul. And Jonathan took off his own coat and gave it to David and gave him his armor, and his sword, and his bow, and his belt. And David went into battle wherever Saul sent him and succeeded so well Saul gave him command over his soldiers, and the people were pleased and so were all the servants of Saul's court.

And it happened as they returned from the slaughter of the Philistines that the women came out of the cities of Israel to meet King Saul with dancing and timbrels and with the three-stringed harps, and they rejoiced and sang, Saul has slain his thousands, and David his ten thousands. This made Saul angry. It seemed to him that it was a wicked saying, and he said, They credit David with ten thousands and me with only thousands! Next thing he'll have the kingdom! From that time on Saul kept an eye on David.

The next day it happened that God's evil spirit overwhelmed Saul in his house and he raved in ecstasy. And David's hand played the lyre as always, but Saul had his spear in his hand and raised the spear and said to himself, I will pin David to the wall. Twice David leaped out of the way. And Saul was afraid of David, because the Lord was with David and had turned against Saul. And Saul sent David far away and made him captain over a thousand. David led the soldiers into battle and out again and everything he did he did well, because the Lord was with him. Saul saw how well everything went for David, and he had a horror of David. But all Israel and Judah loved David, because he led them in and out of battle.

And Saul said to David, Here is my older daughter Merab. I will give her to you to be your wife if you will be my warrior and fight the Lord's battles!—To himself Saul said, It won't be my hand that is lifted against him, but the hand of the Philistines. But David said, Who am I and what is my father's house in Israel that I should become the king's son-in-law? When the time came for Merab to be given to David, she was given in marriage to Adriel the Meholathite instead.

But Saul's daughter Michal loved David, and they told Saul, and he was pleased and said to himself, I will give her to David. She will be the trap that delivers him into the hands of the Philistines. For the second time Saul said to David, To-day you shall become my son-in-law. And Saul commanded the servants of his court to speak privately to David and say, Look, the king likes you, and all the servants of the king's court love you. You should become the king's son-in-law! They spoke these things in David's ear, but David said, Does it seem such a little thing to you, to become the king's son-in-law?

I'm poor, a man of no consequence. They told the king what David had said, and Saul said, Tell David that the king requires no bride price if he will bring him the foreskins of a hundred Philistines and take vengeance on his enemies!—For Saul counted on the hands of the Philistines to kill David for him. The courtiers came and told David what the king had said, and David was pleased to become the king's son-in-law. He waited for nothing but got up and set out with his men and they slew two hundred Philistines and David brought their foreskins to the king and counted them out to him, and Saul gave him his daughter Michal to be his wife.

But Saul knew that the Lord was with David, and that his daughter Michal loved David, and Saul grew more and more afraid of David and was his enemy as long as he lived. Whenever the Philistine princes attacked, David had greater success against them than any of the servants of Saul's court, and his name was held in high regard.

And Saul told his son Jonathan and the servants of his court to kill David. But Saul's son Jonathan loved David very much and told him and said, My father, Saul, wants to kill you. Now, be careful! Tomorrow morning go out and sit in some secret place. Stay hidden. I'll come out and stand beside my father in the field where you are hiding and will talk about you with my father and tell you everything I hear. And so Jonathan praised David to his father and said, Why should the king wrong his servant David, who has never wronged you, and has done you very good service. Didn't he take his life in his hands

when he killed that Philistine? The Lord gave Israel a great victory, and you saw it and rejoiced! Why will you be guilty of innocent blood and kill David for no reason? Saul listened to what Jonathan said and swore an oath and said, As the Lord lives, David shall not die. And Jonathan called David and told him everything the king had said and brought David back to Saul, and David served Saul as he had done before.

There was another war and David fought the Philistines and routed them and they fled from him. And the Lord's evil spirit came upon Saul. Saul sat in his house with his spear in his hand, and David's hand played the lyre. And Saul tried to pin David to the wall with his spear. David leaped out of the way. The spear stuck in the wall and David fled and got away.

But that night Saul sent messengers to watch David's house and kill him in the morning. David's wife, Michal, told her husband and said, Save your life tonight or you'll be dead in the morning! And she let David down by the window, and he ran for his life and got away. Then Michal took the household idol, laid it on the bed, put goat's hair on its head and covered it with a blanket. When Saul's messengers came to seize David, she said, He's ill. Saul sent the messengers back to look for David and said, Bring him to me, bed and all! for Saul wanted David dead. The messengers went in and there was the household idol, in the bed with goat's hair on its head. Why! Saul said to Michal, Why did you betray me? You let my enemy get away! Michal answered, He said to me, Let me go, or do I have to kill you?

▪ ▪

As for David, he got away and fled to Samuel in Ramah and told him everything that Saul had done to him, and he and Samuel stayed in Naioth. When they told Saul that David was at Naioth in Ramah, he sent his messengers to seize David, but the messengers met a group of prophets prophesying in ecstasy, with Samuel at their head, and the spirit of God came upon Saul's messengers and they too began to prophesy. They told Saul and he sent more messengers and they too began to prophesy, and he sent more messengers— the third lot—and they prophesied too. Then Saul went to Ramah himself and came to the great well at Secu and asked, Where are Samuel and David? They said, at Naioth in Ramah. On the way, the spirit of God came upon him too and he walked prophesying as he went and came to Ramah and took off his clothes and prophesyed before Samuel and lay naked all that day and all that night, and that is why people say, Is Saul, too, one of the prophets?

▪ ▪

AND David fled from Ramah and went to Jonathan and said, What have I done? What's the sin that I have committed, or what wrong have I done your father that he wants me dead? Jonathan said, Heaven forbid that you should die! Look, my father never does anything, important or not, without telling me. Why should my father hide something like this from me? It isn't possible. But David said, Your father knows very well how kindly you feel toward me. He'll think, Jonathan mustn't

know, or it will grieve him! As the Lord lives, and as your soul lives, I'm a footfall from my death! Jonathan said, Ask me whatever you want, and I'll do it! David said, Look, tomorrow is the feast of the new moon when I'm to sit in my place at the king's table. Let me hide in the field till the evening of the third day. If your father doesn't see me and misses me, say, David asked me to let him hurry home to Beth-lehem to offer the yearly sacrifice with his family. If he says, That's good! then your servant is safe, but if he becomes angry, you'll know he plans to harm me. Have pity on your servant and remember the covenant of friendship you and I have sworn to each other before the Lord. If you think me guilty, why don't you kill me? Why bring me to your father? Jonathan said, It's the furthest thing from my mind to keep it from you if I see my father plans to harm you! David said, Who will tell me if your father answers you harshly? Jonathan said, Come, Let's walk out in the field! And the two of them went out into the field together. Jonathan said, Let the Lord God of Israel be my witness that around this time tomorrow I'll sound out my father. If he means to harm David, I'll send you word. May God do the same to me and worse if I don't let you know whether my father plans to do you any harm so that you can get away to safety, and may the Lord be with you as He once was with my father. Only show me the Lord's loyal faith so long as I live, and never cut off your loyal faith from my house when the Lord cuts every one of David's enemies from off the earth. Let the name of Jonathan not be cut off from the house of David, and may the Lord avenge David upon his enemies. And Jonathan made David swear his love for him, for he loved David as he loved his own soul.

And Jonathan said, Tomorrow, at the feast of the new moon, your place will be empty and you'll be missed, and you'll be missed more by the third day. Go and hide by the pile of rocks where you hid last time. I'll shoot three arrows as if I were shooting at a mark. Look, I'll send the boy to find them. If I say, They're over on this side, bring them here!—then you can come out and all is well. As the Lord lives, you're in no danger. But if I call after the boy and say, Over there! The arrows are over on the far side!—then run! The Lord is telling you to leave. As for the words that you and I have spoken to each other, let the Lord be our witness forever.

And so David hid in the field, and the new moon came, and the king sat down to break bread. The king sat in his usual seat against the wall. Jonathan sat facing him. Abner took the seat next to Saul, but David's place was empty. Saul said nothing that day. To himself he said, Something has happened to make him unclean, and so he can't come to the table. Next day David's place was still empty, and Saul said, Why has the son of Jesse not come to the table yesterday or today? Jonathan answered, He asked my permission because he wanted very much to go home to Beth-lehem. He said, Please, let me go home. This is the day when my family sacrifices in the town. My brother has sent for me. If you have any kindness for me, let me go and see my brothers!—That's why he hasn't come to the king's table. Now Saul flew into a rage against

Jonathan and said, You son of a rebellious hussy! Don't I know that you're in league with Jesse's son! You shame yourself and shame your mother's nakedness! Don't you understand that as long as the son of Jesse lives upon this earth, neither you nor your kingship will be secure? Go! Send for him and bring him back! He's as good as dead! Jonathan answered his father and said, Why should he die? What has he done? And Saul aimed his spear at Jonathan. Now Jonathan knew his father was determined to kill David and stood up from the table in a fury and would eat no food that second day of the new moon because he was grieved for David and because his father had shamed him.

Early on the third day he went out to the appointed place in the field and took a little boy with him and said, Run and find the arrows I'm going to shoot! The boy ran and Jonathan shot the arrow over the little boy's head and called after him, That arrow is on the far side of you! and called again, Hurry! Be quick about it! Don't hang around there! And the boy picked up Jonathan's arrows and brought them back to his master and suspected nothing and only Jonathan and David knew what it meant. Jonathan gave the weapons to his boy and said, Go, carry them back to town. When the boy was gone, David came out from behind the mound of rocks and fell on his face and prostrated himself three times. They kissed each other and wept together, and it was David who cried the most. Jonathan said, Go in peace! For what you and I have sworn in the Lord's Name, let the Lord be a witness between me and you and between my children and your children forever. Then David set out and went on his way, and Jonathan returned to town.

And David fled to Nob, to the priest Ahimelech. Ahimelech came out to meet David trembling, and said, Why are you alone and without companions? David said, I'm on the king's business and he said no one must know the least thing about it. So I've appointed my men to meet me at such and such a place. Let me have five loaves of bread or whatever you have on hand. The priest said, I don't have any ordinary bread on hand, only holy bread out of the Lord's temple, if your young men have kept away from women. David answered, Women have been kept away from us as always, on any march, even an ordinary one, and much more so today on such a consecrated mission. And so the priest gave him the holy bread, for he had no other bread on hand except the bread one takes from the Lord's presence only when it is replaced with fresh hot bread. Now there happened to be there on that day another man—one of the servants of Saul's court, waiting before the Lord. His name was Doeg, an Edomite, the chief of Saul's herdsmen. And David asked Ahimelech, Don't you have a spear or a sword here somewhere? I didn't bring anything with me—neither my sword nor any other weapon, the king's business was so pressing. The priest said, There's nothing here except the sword of Goliath, the Philistine, whom you slew in the valley of Elah. It's wrapped in the priest's ephod. Take it if you like. We have no other swords here. David said, There's no other sword like it. Give it to me.

On that day David left Saul's domain and fled to Gath, and came to Achish, king of Gath. The servants of the court of Achish said, Isn't that David, the king of the land, the one for whom they dance and sing, Saul has slain his thousands but David his ten thousands? David took their words to heart, and was very much afraid of King Achish of Gath, and so he acted the madman, raved in front of them and drummed on doors and let spittle run down his beard. Achish said, Can't you see that the man is mad? Why have you brought him to me? Don't I have enough madmen in Gath? Why do you bring me this fellow to rave in my house?

And David left and fled to the cave of Adullam. When his brothers and all his father's house heard, they came to him. And all kinds of men gathered about him —men who were in trouble or in need or in debt—an embittered lot of souls—and he became their leader. He soon had with him some four hundred men. From there David went on to Mizpah in Moab and said to the king of Moab, Please let my father and my mother settle safely here among you until I know what God means to do with me. And he brought them to the king of Moab and they lived in the land of Moab as long as David stayed in his mountain stronghold. But the prophet Gad spoke to David and said, Don't stay in your stronghold but get yourself down into the land of Judah. So David left and came to the forest of Hereth.

Saul heard about David and his band of men and learned his whereabouts. Saul was in Gibeah sitting on a hill under a tamarisk tree and had his spear in his hand, with the servants of his court standing around him. And Saul said, Listen, you Benjaminites! Has Jesse's son given each of you fields and vineyards? Is he going to make you captains over hundreds and thousands? I know you! You are, all of you, in the plot against me! Not one of you has come to tell me my son is in league with the son of Jesse! Not one of you pities me and comes and tells me in my ear when my son stirs up my servant to rebel against me or that they lie in ambush for me this very day! Now Doeg the Edomite was standing among the servants of Saul's court and said, I saw the son of Jesse at Nob, when he came to the priest Ahimelech son of Ahitub, who questioned the Lord for him and gave him food, and gave him the sword of Goliath the Philistine. And so the king sent for the priest Ahimelech, son of Ahitub, and all his father's house, the priests who were in Nob, and they all came and stood before the king. Saul said, Listen, you son of Ahitub! And he said, Here I am, my lord. Saul said, Why do you plot against me—you and the son of Jesse? You gave him bread and a sword and questioned God for him! You stirred him up against me and you're lying in ambush for me this very today! Ahimelech answered him and said, Who among your servants is there like David, your own son-in-law, a trusted officer, commander of your bodyguard, honored in your household? Is this the first time that I have questioned the Lord for him? May the king find no fault in his servant or in any one of my father's house in any matter great or small, because your servant knew nothing about any of this. But the king said, You, Ahimelech, are going to die, yes, you and all your father's house! And to his bodyguards, who stood about him, the king said, Surround them!

Kill the priests of the Lord, for they have given David their hand. They knew that he was fleeing and they didn't tell me! But the king's men would not raise their hands to strike the Lord's priests.

Now the king said, And you, Doeg, will you step forward and strike the priests? And Doeg the Edomite stepped forward, and it was he who struck down the priests. He killed eighty-five men in their priestly robes that day, and in the priestly City of Nob, too, he put to the sword men and women, the children at play and babies at the breast, the oxen and asses and sheep. Only one of the sons of Ahimelech son of Ahitub escaped and fled to David. He was Abiathar and he told David that Saul had killed the priests of the Lord. David said, I knew it, that day when I saw Doeg the Edomite there! I was sure he would tell Saul! I am the cause of all the deaths in your father's house! Stay with me. Don't be afraid. He who seeks your life seeks my life too. You'll be safe with me here.

▪▪

THEY told David, Look, the Philistines attack the gates of Keilah and plunder the threshing floors. David questioned the Lord and asked, Shall I go and fight these Philistines? The Lord said, Go, fight them and save Keilah. But David's men said, Look, we are afraid here, in Judah! What will happen to us if we go to Keilah against the armies of the Philistines? And David questioned and asked the Lord again, and the Lord answered, Go on down to Keilah. I will deliver the Philistines into your hand! And so David and his men went to Keilah and fought the Philistines and drove away their cattle and routed them and David saved the inhabitants of Keilah.

Now when Abiathar came to David, he had brought the priestly ephod with him.

When they told Saul that David had come to Keilah, he said, God has sold him into my hand. He has entered a city with gates and bolts, and locked himself in! And Saul called the army to the battle and to go down to Keilah and besiege David and his men. When David understood the mischief that Saul planned against him, he called Abiathar the priest and said, Bring the priestly ephod here! And David said, Lord, God of Israel, Your servant has heard that Saul is on his way to Keilah to destroy the city because of me. Tell me, O Lord, God of Israel, if it is true, what your servant has heard: Is Saul on his way down? The Lord said, He is on his way down. And David asked, Is it true that the lords of Keilah will hand me and my men over to Saul? The Lord said, They will hand you over. And so David and his men—some six hundred of them—hurried away from Keilah and went this way and that, wherever they could go. When Saul heard that David had escaped from Keilah, he gave up his march.

David remained in the strongholds and lived in the hills in the wilderness of Ziph, and Saul searched for him day in, day out, but God did not deliver him into Saul's hand. And David knew Saul was searching for him and meant to kill him, and he remained in the forests of the wilderness of Ziph. And Saul's son Jonathan came and found David in the forest and encouraged him in his trust in God and said, Don't be afraid! My father Saul will never find you. It is you who will be king of Israel, and I

will be second to you, and my father Saul knows it! And the two of them made a covenant with each other before the Lord and David remained in the forest, and Jonathan went home.

But certain Ziphites went to Saul in Gibeah and said, David is among us, hiding in the mountain strongholds in the forest on Mount Hachilah, south of Jeshimon. Now if my lord the king will be pleased to come down, come, and we shall make it our business to deliver him into my lord the king's hands! Saul said, May the Lord bless you because you have pity on me! And he said, You go ahead and keep your eyes open. Keep a look out and make sure you know where his foot comes to rest and who has sighted him. They tell me he is very cunning. Keep watch and spy out every secret place where he hides out. When you are sure, come back and tell me and I'll go with you. If he is anywhere in the land, I'll run him down among all the clans in Judah. And so they set out and went to Ziph ahead of Saul. And David and his men were in the wilderness of Maon in the Arabah south of Jeshimon.

When they told David that Saul and his men were coming after him, he made his way down the side of the crag which was in the wilderness of Maon, and Saul heard and chased David into the wilderness of Maon, and Saul came around one side of the mountain, and David and his men around the other hurrying to escape from Saul, and Saul and his men were about to encircle and capture David and his men when there came a messenger to Saul saying, Come, quickly! The Philistines are attacking the land! And Saul stopped chasing David to march against the Philistines. And that is why that place is called Sela-hammahlekoth, which means rock of parting.

From there David went up and settled in the mountain strongholds of En-gedi. And it happened that when Saul returned from his pursuit of the Philistines they said to him, Look, David is in the wilderness of En-gedi. Saul picked three thousand of the best men of Israel to go in search of David and his men among the Cliffs of Wild Goats, and Saul came to some sheepfolds beside the road and there was a cave and he went inside to relieve himself. Now in the back of the cave sat David and his men. David's men said, Look! The Lord promised there would come a day when He would deliver your enemy into your hands, and this is the day! You can do with him whatever you like! And David took his sword and got up quietly and cut off a corner of Saul's coat. But afterward his heart beat because he had cut off a corner of Saul's coat! To his men he said, God forbid that I should have done such a thing and laid hands on my lord, the Lord's anointed, for he is the anointed of the Lord! With these words David restrained his men and would not let them rise against Saul. But when Saul got up and left the cave and went on his way, David got up too and came out of the cave behind him and called after Saul and said, My lord the king! Saul looked behind him, and David bowed down with his forehead to the ground and prostrated himself and said, Why do you listen to the talk of the men who say, Look, David is out to hurt you? Today your eyes have seen how the Lord delivered you into my hands inside the cave, and though my people urged me to kill you, I pitied you. I said, I will not lay hands on my lord, for he is the Lord's anointed. Look, my father, at the corner of your coat in my hand! I cut off a corner of your coat when I could have killed you. Can't you see that my hands are clean of any malice or harm! I've done you no wrong and yet you hunt me and want to take my life! The Lord will judge between me and you, and will avenge me; but my hand will not touch you. There's an old saying that wickedness proceeds from wicked men, but I will not raise my hand against you. Whom does the king of Israel chase and whom do you hunt? A dead dog? A single flea? The Lord be the judge and find justly between you and me! May He plead my plea and judge for me against you!

When David finished speaking, Saul said, Is that your voice, my son David?— and he wept aloud and said, You are more just than I. You have done me good, who have done you harm. You have shown me your goodness today when the Lord handed me over to you and you did not kill me. What man finds his enemy and lets him go safely away? The Lord will repay you the good that you have done me today. Look, I know that it is you who will be king, and that the kingship of Israel will be established by your hand! Now swear to me, in the name of the Lord, that you will not root out my seed after me, nor wipe my name out of my father's house. And David swore Saul an oath, and Saul went home to his house, and David and his men climbed back up into the stronghold.

▪ ▪

AND Samuel died, and all Israel gathered and mourned him, and they buried him at his house in Ramah.

And David moved down to the wilderness of Paran. Now there was a man in Maon, whose business was in Carmel, a very rich man. He had three thousand sheep and a thousand goats, and it happened that he was shearing his sheep in Carmel. His name was Nabal and his wife's name was Abigail, a woman of good sense and beauty. But the man was rough and mean—a Calebite. Out in the wilderness David heard that Nabal was shearing his sheep and sent ten of his young men to him and said to them, Go up to Nabal in Carmel. Greet him in my name and say, Peace to you and to your household and all that belongs to you. I hear that you are

shearing. Now your shepherds have been out here with us, and we have never done them any harm. Was there anything of theirs missing in all the time they were in Carmel? Ask your young men and they will tell you. Therefore be kind to these young men for we come on a festival. Please give your servants and your son David anything you have on hand. David's young men came to Nabal and said all these things to him in David's name and then they waited quietly, but Nabal said, Who is this David? Who's this son of Jesse? There are a lot of servants these days who run away from their masters! Should I take my bread and my wine and the meat I've slaughtered for my own sheepshearers and give it to men who come from I don't know where? And David's young men turned around and went back and told him everything. David said, Let each man gird on his sword—and each man girded his sword on, and David too girded on his sword, and there were some four hundred men who went with David, and two hundred remained behind with their belongings.

But one of the young men told Abigail, Nabal's wife, and said, Look, David sent messengers out of the wilderness to greet our master and he shouted at them! And yet these men were very good to us and never did us any harm, nor did we lose a thing all the time we were out in the open fields with them. They were a wall around us night and day, all the time we were with them tending the flocks. You had better think and decide what to do, because there's a disaster in store for our master and all his household. As for him—he's a mean fellow and nobody dares say anything to him. Abigail quickly took two hundred loaves of bread, two skins of wine, five dressed sheep, five measures of roasted corn, a hundred raisin cakes, and two hundred fig cakes, loaded them onto the asses and said to her young men, Go on ahead of me. Look, I'll be right behind

you. But she said nothing about it to her husband Nabal. As she came riding down the mountain path on her ass, look, here came David and his men down toward her and so they met each other.

Now David had said to himself, Was it all for nothing that I guarded everything this fellow had in the wilderness, so that nothing was lost of all he had, and he repays me evil for good? May God do the same and worse to David if I leave a single one who pisses against the wall out of all his household alive to see the sun come up tomorrow morning! When Abigail saw David, she quickly got down from the ass, bowed with her forehead to the ground, and fell at his feet, and said, Ah, my lord, let the blame be mine! Listen, I beg you, to what your maidservant says in your ear and hear your servant's words! Oh, let my lord pay no attention to that abominable man, Nabal, for he is what his name says: His name means boor and a boor is what he is! As for me—your maidservant never saw the young men whom my lord sent to us. And now, my lord, as the Lord lives, and as you live, it is the Lord who has kept you from shedding blood and taking vengeance with your own hand. May your enemies and all who wish my lord harm end up as Nabal is going to end up. As for the blessing of this gift which your maidservant has brought for my lord, let it be given to the young men who follow at my lord's heels. Forgive, if you please, your servant's wickedness. There is no doubt that the Lord will make my lord an enduring house because my lord fights the Lord's battles, nor shall any harm be found in you all the days of your life. If any man should rise to pursue you and seek your life, then my lord's life will be bound in the bond of life with the Lord your God, but your enemies' life will be slung like shot from a sling. When the Lord fulfills his good promise to my lord and makes you prince of Israel, let it not be a stumbling block nor an impediment in my lord's heart to have been guilty of shedding needless blood because my lord has avenged himself with his own hand! And when the Lord shows my lord His goodness, may you remember your maidservant!

David said, Blessed is the Lord, the God of Israel, who sent you to meet me on this day, and a blessing on your wisdom, and a blessing on you, for today you have saved me from shedding blood and taking vengeance by my own hand. By the life of the Lord, God of Israel, who has kept me from doing you harm, if you had not hurried to meet me, not one in Nabal's household who pisses against the wall would have lived to see the sun come up tomorrow morning. And David took from her hand what she had brought him, and said, Go home in peace! I have heard your words. Rise up! Look, I'll do what you say.

When Abigail came home to Nabal, there he was in the house, feasting at a feast fit for a king, in high spirits and very drunk, so that she said nothing one way or the other to him till next morning when it grew light. But in the morning, when he had slept off the wine, his wife told him everything and his heart died within him and he lay like a stone. Ten days later the Lord struck Nabal dead.

When David heard that Nabal was dead, he said, Blessed be the Lord who has avenged the insult against me and saved His servant from evil! He has turned Nabal's evil deed back upon his own head. And David sent word to Abigail that he would take her to be his wife. David's young men came to Abigail at Carmel and spoke with her and said, David has sent us to you, so that he may take you to be his wife. Abigail rose and bowed down with her face to the ground and said, Look, Here stands your maidservant, a slave willing to wash the feet of my lord's servants! And Abigail got up quickly and mounted her ass, and her five young women came behind her and she followed David's messengers and became his wife.

David had also taken Ahinoam of Jezreel to be his wife, and they both became his wives. As for David's wife, Saul's daughter Michal, Saul had given her to Palti, son of Laish from Gallim.

． ．

AND the Ziphites came to Saul at Gibeah and said, David is hiding on the hill of Hachilah, across from Jeshimon. And Saul set out and went down to the wilderness of Ziph with three thousand of the best men of Israel to hunt for David in the wilderness of Ziph. Saul encamped beside the road on the hill of Hachilah, across from Jeshimon. David was living in the wilderness. When he heard that Saul had come into the wilderness after him, he sent out spies to learn if it was true. And David set out and came to the place where Saul was encamped and saw Saul lying beside Abner son of Ner, the commander of Saul's army. As for Saul, he lay well inside the camp with soldiers all around him. And David said to Ahimelech, the Hittite, and to Abishai son of Zeruiah, Joab's brother, Who will go down to Saul with me into the camp? Abishai said, I'll go with you. And so David and Abishai went down by night, and there lay Saul asleep well inside the camp with his spear stuck into the ground by his head, with Abner and the soldiers lying all around him. Now Abishai said, This is the day on which God has delivered your enemy into your hand. Just let me pin him to the ground here and now. One thrust with his own spear, and I won't need a second. But David said, You must not do him any harm! Who can lift a hand against the Lord's anointed and go unpunished? And he said, As the Lord lives, the Lord will strike him down, or his time will come and he will die, or he will fall in battle and be no more. God forbid that I should raise my hand against the Lord's anointed. But take the spear that is by his head and the jug of water, and let's go! And so David took the spear and the jug from where they stood at his head and they went away, and nobody saw or knew it or woke up. They all slept on, for a deep sleep from the Lord had fallen upon them.

When David got to the other side, he went and stood up on top of the hill, and there was a great distance between them, and he called to the soldiers and to Abner son of Ner, and said, Abner! Why don't you answer me? Abner answered, Who are you, to be shouting at the king? David said, Are you a man or no? There's not another man like you in Israel, right? So why don't you keep watch over your lord the king? One of our soldiers came to murder your lord the king! You're not doing very well, are you? As the Lord lives, the whole lot of you deserve to die for not keeping watch over your lord, the Lord's anointed! Look over here! Here's the king's spear and the jug of water that stood by his head. Saul knew David's voice and said, Is that your voice, David, my son? David said, It is my voice, my lord and king! And then he said, Why does my lord hunt his servant? What have I done? What evil is there in my hand? If only my lord and king will listen to his servant's words! If it is the Lord who stirs you up against me, may my sacrifice smell acceptably to him! But if they are men, then may they be cursed in the sight of the Lord, for today they have banished me from my share in the Lord's inheritance and have said, Go serve other gods! May my blood not fall far from the Lord's presence! The king of Israel has come out to find one flea, as if he were hunting a partridge in the mountains. And Saul said, I have sinned! Come back, my son David! I will not do you any more harm, for today you have shown a value for my life! Look, I have been a fool and have done wrong. David answered and said, Look, here is my lord the king's spear. Let one of the young men come over and get it. May the Lord repay every man his righteousness and loyalty. The Lord delivered you into my hand, but I would not lay my hand on the Lord's anointed. As I have valued your life today, may the Lord value my life and save me from every peril! Then Saul said, Blessings on you, my son David. You will undertake great things and will succeed. And David went on his way and Saul returned home.

▪ ▪

AND in his heart David said, The day will come when I must fall into Saul's hand. It is best that I escape into the land of the Philistines. Saul will despair of finding me within the borders of Israel and I will escape his hand. And David set out, and he and his six hundred men went over to Achish son of Maoch, king of Gath. And David remained with Achish in Gath, he and his men with their households, and David with his two wives Ahinoam, the Jezreelite, and Abigail, the wife of Nabal, of Carmel. When Saul heard that David had fled to Gath, he stopped hunting him.

Now David said to King Achish, If you want to show me a kindness, let them give me a place to live in one of the towns in the country, so I can settle there. Why should your servant live here with you in the king's city? And that day Achish gave him Ziklag. That is why Ziklag belongs to the kings of Judah to this day. The time David spent in the land of the Philistines was a year and four months. David and his men would go out and raid the Geshurites and the Gizrites and the Amalekites, who had always lived in the region, as far as Shur and up to the land of Egypt. Whenever David and his men raided the land, they left neither man nor woman alive and carried off their sheep and oxen and asses and the camels and clothing and returned home. If he came to Achish and Achish asked him, Where did you raid today? David would say, In the southland of Judah and the southland of the Jerahmeelites, or the southland of the Kenites. And David left not a man or woman alive to bring the story to Gath, for he said, They might betray us and say, This and this is what David did while he lived in the land of the Philistines! But Achish believed David and said to himself, He has made himself hated by his people in Israel and will be my slave forever.

And it happened in those days that the Philistines gathered their army for battle against Israel. And Achish said to David, Know that you're going to go out into the field with me—you and your men! David said to Achish, Well then you will see what your servant shall do! And Achish said, I'll make you my bodyguard for all the days of your life.

..

AND Samuel had died and all Israel mourned him and buried him in his own city of Ramah. And Saul had banished the sorcerers and all who call up spirits out of the land. But now the Philistines gathered and made camp at Shunem, and Saul gathered the army of Israel and made camp in Gilboa. When Saul saw the Philistine army, he was terrified and his heart trembled. Saul questioned the Lord, but the Lord did not answer him, not in dreams, nor by the lot Urim, nor through the prophets. And Saul said to his servants, Find me a woman who can call up spirits, so that I can go to her and question her. His men said, Look, there's a woman in En-dor who can call up spirits. And Saul disguised himself and put on different clothes and set out—he and two of his men—and they came to the woman in the night. Saul said, Divine for me, please, by a spirit and raise me up the one whom I will name to you. The woman said, Look, you know yourself that Saul has banished sorcerers and those who call up spirits out

of the land. Are you laying a trap to have me put to death? But Saul swore in the name of the Lord and said, As the Lord lives, you shall not be held guilty in this matter. The woman said, Whom shall I call up for you? He said, Call up Samuel! Now when the woman understood that this concerned Samuel, she screamed and said, Why do you deceive me? You are Saul! The king said, Don't be afraid! Tell me what you see! She said, I see a spirit rising out of the earth. He said, What does he look like? She said, An old man rising wrapped in a linen robe. And Saul knew that it was Samuel and bowed down with his forehead to the ground and prostrated himself.

But Samuel said, Why do you disturb my rest and make me come up here? Saul said, Because I am in trouble. The Philistines fight with me and God has turned away and does not answer me—not by prophecy nor in dreams. That's why I have had you called to tell me what to do! Samuel said, Why ask me, now that the Lord has turned away from you and become your enemy? The Lord has done what He told me to tell you that He would do. He has torn the kingdom out of your hand and given it to your neighbor David, because you did not obey the Lord and did not execute his fury upon Amalek! That is why the Lord has done what He has done to you today. That is why the Lord will give you, and Israel too, into the hands of the Philistines. Tomorrow you and your sons will be here with me and the Lord will give Israel into the hands of the Philistines!

Now Saul fell full-length to the ground overcome with horror at Samuel's words. All his strength was gone, because he had eaten no food the whole day and the whole night. And the woman came to Saul and saw how very frightened he was and said, Look, your servant listened to your voice; I took my life into my hands when I heard your words. Now you must listen to your maidservant's voice. I will bring you a bite of bread. Eat and get your strength back before you go on your way. He refused and said, I will not eat, but his servants and the woman urged him until he listened to what they said and got up from the ground and sat on the bed. The woman had a fattened calf in the house. She quickly butchered it and took flour and kneaded it and baked unleavened bread and set it before Saul and his men, and when they had eaten, they got up and left that same night.

■ ■

BUT the Philistines assembled all their forces at Aphek, and Israel made camp by the spring in Jezreel. And the princes of the Philistines marched with their companies of hundreds and thousands, and David and his men marched in the rear with Achish. The Philistine captains said to Achish, What are those Hebrews doing here? Achish said, Isn't this the same David, the servant of Saul, king of Israel, who's been with me for more than a year? I've never found any fault in him from the day he defected to me to this day. But

the Philistine captains became angry with him and said, Send the fellow away! Make him go back to the place you assigned him so he will not go into battle with us, for he might turn against us. What better way for this fellow to get back into his lord's favor than with the heads of our men? Isn't this the same David for whom they danced their dances and sang, Saul has slain his thousands, and David his tens of thousands? And so Achish called David and said, As the Lord lives, you are a man of honor, and I would like to have you with me in the comings and goings of battle, for I have found no fault in you from the day you came to me to this day. But the Philistine princes don't like you, therefore turn back. Go in peace, so you will not do wrong in the eyes of the Philistine princes. David said, What have I done? What wrong has your servant done from the day I entered your service to this day? Why may I not go and fight the enemies of my lord the king? Achish said, I think you are good as an angel of God, but the Philistine captains say, he shall not march into battle with us! So now, get up early in the morning—you and your lord's men, who have come with you. Get up early in the morning and go back to the place I have given you as soon as day breaks. So David and his men got up early in the morning to go back to the land of the Philistines, and the Philistines marched up to Jezreel.

■ ■

Now David and his men arrived in Ziklag on the third day. The Amalekites had been raiding the southlands and had come to

Ziklag and struck Ziklag and set it on fire. They had taken the women and everybody, young and old, captive. They had killed no one but had gone on their way and taken them along. David and his men entered the city and saw that it had been set on fire and their wives and their sons and their daughters taken captive. David and his men wept aloud until they had no strength to weep. David's two wives, Ahinoam of Jezreel, and Abigail, the widow of Nabal, of Carmel, had been taken captive too. And now David was in trouble. His men wanted to stone him in their grief, for each man's heart was bitter at the loss of his sons and his daughters. But David strengthened himself in the Lord, his God. He said to the priest Abiathar son of Ahimelech, Bring me the ephod! Abiathar brought him the ephod, and David asked the Lord and said, Should I chase after these raiders? Can I overtake them? He said, Chase after them, for you will overtake them and free the captives. And so David and his six hundred men set out and came to the wadi of Besor. And David and four hundred men continued the chase, but two hundred of the men were tired out and did not cross the wadi of Besor but stayed behind.

They found an Egyptian in the field and brought him to David. They gave him bread to eat and water to drink, and dried figs, and he ate and his spirit revived, because he had had no food or drink for three days and three nights. Then David said, To whom do you belong? Where are you from? He said, I am a young Egyptian, the slave of an Amalekite. My master left me behind three days ago when I fell ill. We had raided the Cherethites in the south

and the southern borders of Judah and southern Caleb and set Ziklag on fire. David said, Can you take me to this band? He said, Swear to me by God that you won't kill me or hand me over to my master, and I will lead you down to this band. So he led him down, and there they were, sprawled over the ground, eating and drinking and celebrating the great plunder they had taken from the land of the Philistines and Judah. And David battered them from the first light of dawn until the evening of the next day, and no one escaped except the four hundred young men who got on their camels and fled.

David recovered everything that the Amalekites had taken and rescued his own two wives. No one was missing from the

youngest to the oldest, neither sons nor daughters, none of the plunder, nor anything that they had taken. David recovered everything, and he took the sheep and the cattle and drove them before him and said, This is David's spoil! When David came to the wadi of Besor, the two hundred men who had been tired out and had not followed came to meet David and the men who had gone with him, and David gave them a friendly greeting. But the bad and godless among the men who had gone with David said, They didn't go with us, so we won't share the spoils that we recovered, except to give each man his own wife and children. Let them go their ways. But David said, That, my brothers, is not the way to treat what the Lord has given us! He has watched over us and delivered this band that had overcome us into our hands! Why should we listen to you? He who goes to battle and he who guards the gear shall have an equal part. They shall share alike. And that has been the statute and custom in Israel from that day to this.

When David returned to Ziklag, he sent portions of the spoils to the elders of Judah, saying, Here's a present for you out of the spoils from the enemies of the Lord! He sent portions to those in Beth-el, and to those in Ramoth-negeb, and those in Jattir, and to those in Aroer, to those in Siphmoth, to those in Eshtemoa, to those in Racal, to those in the cities of the Jerahmeelites, to those in the cities of the Kenites, to those in Hormah, to those in Bor-ashan, to those in Athach, to those in Hebron, and to all the places where David had gone in and out with his men.

• •

BUT the Philistines fought against Israel, and the men of Israel fled from the Philistines and the fallen lay dead on Mount Gilboa. And the Philistines closed in on Saul and his sons and they slew Saul's sons Jonathan, and Abinadab, and Malchishua. The battle raged and the archers found Saul and an arrow pierced his belly. As he lay wounded, he said to his arms-

bearer, Draw your sword and run me through, before those uncircumcised louts can run me through and play their games with me. But his arms-bearer would not because he was very much afraid. And Saul took the sword and fell upon it. When his arms-bearer saw that Saul was dead, he fell upon his sword too and died with him.

Thus Saul and his three sons, and his arms-bearer, and all his men died on the same day. When the people of Israel on the far side of the valley and in the valley of Jordan saw the army of Israel in flight and heard that Saul and his sons were dead, they deserted their cities and fled, and the Philistines came and lived in them. Next day the Philistines came to strip the slain and found Saul and his three sons where they had fallen on Mount Gilboa. They cut off Saul's head and stripped him of his armor and sent the good news throughout Philistia to gladden their gods and all the people. And they put his armor in the temple of Ashtaroth, and his corpse they hung on the wall of Beth-shan. But the men of Jabesh-gilead heard what the Philistines had done to Saul, and a band of warriors set out and they traveled all night and took down Saul's corpse and the corpses of his sons from the wall of Beth-shan and brought them back to Jabesh, and there they burned them and took their bones and buried them under the tamarisk in Jabesh and fasted seven days.

• •

ON the third day after Saul's death, when David had returned from the fight with the Amalekites and had been back in Zik-

lag for two days, look, here came a man out of Saul's camp with his clothes torn and earth on his head. He came to David and bowed down and prostrated himself. David said, Where do you come from? He said, I have escaped out of the camp of Israel. David said, Tell me how it went. He said, The army has fled the battle. Many have fallen and are dead, and Saul is dead too, and his son Jonathan. And David asked the young man who had told him this, How do you know that Saul and his son Jonathan are dead?

The young man who told him this said, By chance! I chanced to be on Mount Gilboa and look! there was Saul, leaning onto his spear with the chariots and horsemen closing in! He looked around and saw me and called to me. I said, Here I am. He said, Who are you? I said, I'm an Amalekite. He said, Come here and kill me! Pain has me in its grip and yet life won't let go of me! So I went to him and killed him because I knew he could not live after his fall. Then I took the crown off his head and the bracelet from his arm and have brought them to you, my lord. And David took hold of his clothes and tore them, and so did all his people. And they mourned and wept and fasted until evening for Saul and for his son Jonathan, and for the people of the Lord and the whole house of Israel because they had fallen by the sword. But to the young man who had told him this, David said, Where do you come from? He said, I am the son of a

stranger, an Amalekite, who lives in this land. David said, How is it that you were not afraid to raise your hand to annihilate the Lord's anointed? And David called one of his men and said, Come here and strike him down! And he struck him down so that he died. David said, Your blood is upon your head because your own mouth has testified against you when you said, I have slain the Lord's anointed.

And David lamented this lamentation over Saul and his son Jonathan and said, Teach the children of Judah the Song of the Bow. Look, it is written in the Book of the Just.

The glory of Israel lies slain upon your mountains! How the mighty have fallen!

Never tell it in Gath, nor proclaim it in the streets of Ashkelon, or our enemy's daughters will rejoice, the daughters of the uncircumcised will triumph!

You mountains of Gilboa, let there be no dew and no rain upon you, nor the fruit of the field, for this is where the shield of warriors was thrown down, the shield of Saul, as if it had not been anointed with oil!

Jonathan's bow never failed him, nor did Saul's sword come back empty without the blood of the slain or the fat of a fallen hero.

Saul and Jonathan, lovely and beloved in their lives, were not parted in their deaths.

They were faster than eagles, they were stronger than lions.

You daughters of Israel, weep for Saul who clothed you in costly crimson, with golden ornaments upon your dresses!

How the mighty have fallen in the midst of battle!

Jonathan is slain upon your heights! I grieve for you, my brother Jonathan! You have been very lovely to me! Your love for me was more wonderful than the love of women.

How the mighty have fallen, how the weapons of war are lost!

∎ ∎

SOON afterward, David went to the Lord and asked Him, Shall I go up to one of the towns of Judah? The Lord said, Go up! David said, Where shall I go? The Lord said, To Hebron. David went up with his

two wives, Ahinoam, the Jezreelite, and Abigail, the wife of Nabal, the Carmelite. And David took the men, each with his family, and they settled in the towns around Hebron. And the men of Judah came and anointed David king of the house of Judah.

When they told David that the men of Jabesh-gilead had buried Saul, he sent messengers to them to say, The Lord bless you because you have been faithful to your lord Saul and buried him. Now may the Lord be merciful and faithful to you, and I too will return you kindness for your kindness. Make yourselves strong and be brave, for your lord Saul is dead and the house of Judah has anointed me to be their king.

∙ ∙

BUT Abner son of Ner, who had been commander of Saul's army, took Saul's son Ish-bosheth and brought him to Mahanaim and made him king of Gilead, Ashur, Jezreel, Ephraim, and Benjamin, and of all Israel. Saul's son Ish-bosheth was forty years old when he became king of Israel and he reigned for two years. Only the house of Judah followed David. But it was seven years and six months that David reigned in Hebron as king over the house of Judah.

And Abner son of Ner led the army of Saul's son Ish-bosheth from Mahanaim to Gibeon, and Joab son of Zeruiah led David's army, and they met by the pond of Gibeon and made camp, one on one side of the pond, and the other on the other side. And Abner called to Joab and said, Let the young men play war games for

us. Joab said, Yes, let them. And so they counted twelve young men of the party of Benjamin and Saul's son Ish-bosheth, and twelve of David's young men, and each took hold of his adversary's head and thrust his sword in his adversary's side and they all fell together. That is why the place is called Helkath-hazzurim, meaning field of the flints, and it is near Gibeon.

There ensued a fierce battle that day, and Abner and the army of Israel were beaten by David's men. Among them were the three sons of Zeruiah: Joab, Abishai, and Asahel. Asahel was light-footed and fast as a deer in the field. He chased after Abner and kept chasing him, turning neither right nor left. Abner looked behind him and said, Is that you, Asahel? And he said, Yes. Abner said, Turn right or turn left and grab yourself one of the young men and take his armor! But Asahel didn't turn aside and wouldn't stop chasing after him. Again Abner said, Stop chasing me! I don't want to have to cut you down to the ground. How could I ever face your brother Joab? But Asahel refused to turn aside, and Abner ran him through the belly with the back of his spear so that it came out the other side, and he fell and died on the spot, and whoever passed the spot where Asahel lay dead stood still.

But Joab and Abishai chased after Abner. The sun was going down as they reached Mount Ammah across from Giah on the road to the wilderness of Gibeon. And the Benjaminites massed behind Abner and stood at the top of the hill, and Abner called to Joab and said, Why should the sword go on devouring us forever? Don't you know this will end in nothing but more misery? When will you tell your soldiers to stop chasing after their brothers? Joab said, As God lives, if you had only said this in the morning, we could all have disbanded and not a single soldier would have chased after his brother! And Joab sounded the horn, and his soldiers stood still and stopped hunting the men of Israel, and they stopped fighting.

Abner and his men walked along the Jordan Valley all that night, crossed over the Jordan, and traversed all of Bithron until they came to Mahanaim. After Joab stopped hunting Abner, he mustered his army, and nineteen of David's men were missing besides Asahel. But David's men had killed three hundred and sixty Benjaminites of Abner's army. They took up Asahel and buried him in his father's grave in Beth-lehem. And Joab and his men marched all that night, and the dawn broke for them at Hebron.

It was a long war between the house of Saul and the house of David, and David grew stronger and stronger, and the house of Saul grew weaker. And sons were born to David in Hebron. His firstborn was Amnon, by Ahinoam, the Jezreelite; the second was Chileab, by Abigail, the wife of Nabal the Carmelite; the third was Absalom, the son of Maacah, the daughter of Talmai, king of Geshur; the fourth, Adonijah, was the son of Haggith; the fifth, Shephatiah, the son of Abital; the sixth was Ithream by David's wife Eglah. They were born to David in Hebron.

▪ ▪

THROUGHOUT the war between the house of Saul and the house of David, Abner's power grew in the house of Saul. Now

Saul had a concubine called Rizpah, a daughter of Aiah, and Saul's son Ish-bosheth asked Abner, Why did you lie with my father's concubine? Ish-bosheth's words so enraged Abner he said, Am I some dog's head out of Judah, I, who have been loyal to your father Saul's house, and his kin, and his friends, I, who have saved you from falling into David's hands? And today you are accusing me because of a woman! May God do the same and worse to Abner if I don't accomplish for David what the Lord has promised him and take the kingship from the house of Saul and establish David on the throne of Israel and Judah from Dan as far as Beer-sheba! And he had not a word with which to answer Abner, because he was afraid of him.

Now Abner sent messengers to David to say, Whose land shall it be? Look, make a covenant with me and I'll help you and bring all Israel over to your side! David said, Good. I'll make a covenant with you, but there's one condition. When you come before my face, you're not going to see my face unless you bring me Saul's daughter Michal. And David sent messengers to Saul's son Ish-bosheth, to say, Give me my wife Michal for whom I paid the bride price of one hundred Philistine foreskins. And Ish-bosheth sent to have her taken away from her husband Paltiel son of Laish, and her husband went with her, and walked weeping behind her as far as Bahurim where Abner said, Turn back, and he turned back. And Abner spoke with the elders of Israel and said, You have always wanted David to be your king. Now do it, for the Lord has said, By the hand of My servant David will I deliver My people Israel out of the hand of the Philistines and out of the hand of all their enemies. Abner said the same thing to the Benjaminites. Then he went to David in Hebron and let him know the wishes of Israel and of all the house of Benjamin. David made a feast for Abner and the twenty men who had come to Hebron with him. And Abner said, I'll go and gather all of Israel to my lord the king. They will make a covenant with you, and you shall reign to your heart's content. And David dismissed Abner so that he could leave safely.

And look, here came Joab and David's men returning from a raid, bringing home a lot of plunder, but Abner had left Hebron, for David had dismissed him so that he could leave safely. When they told Joab and his soldiers how Abner son of Ner had come to the king and that he had dismissed him and let him leave safely, Joab went to the king and said, Look what you've done! Abner comes to you, and you let him leave safely! Why? Now he's gone! Don't you know Abner son of Ner? He came to trick you and to spy out your comings and goings and to find out all about you. Joab left David and sent messengers after Abner, and they brought him back from Bor-sirah, and David knew nothing about it. Now when Abner returned to Hebron, Joab took him aside as for a private talk inside the gate, and there he struck him in the belly so that Abner died for the shedding of his brother Asahel's blood.

Afterward when David heard about it, he said, I and my kingdom are forever innocent before the Lord of the blood of Abner son of Ner. Let the guilt be upon Joab's head and on all his father's house. May the house of Joab never be without a man with a discharge, or a leper, or a man at a spindle, or one who dies by the sword, or lacks bread. Joab and his brother Abishai murdered Abner because he killed their brother Asahel in the battle at Gibeon. And to Joab and to all his soldiers David said, Tear your clothes! Put on sackcloth and walk mourning in front of Abner's bier! And King David walked behind it. They buried Abner in Hebron, and the king lifted his voice and wept by Abner's grave, and the soldiers wept too. The king lamented Abner and said, Why should Abner die like a criminal? Your hands were not bound nor your feet laid in chains, yet you fell like one falling before wicked men! And the people wept more. David's men came and urged him to eat while it was still day, but David swore an oath and said, May God do the same to me and worse if I taste bread or anything else before the sun sets. And the soldiers liked what they saw, as they liked everything the king did. All the army and all Israel understood that it was not by the king's wish that Abner son of Ner had been killed. And the king spoke to the servants of his court and said, Don't you know that today a prince and a great man has fallen in Israel? I am a weak man today even though I am the anointed king. These men—these sons of Zeruiah—are too hard for me! May the Lord repay the wicked according to their wickedness. When Saul's son Ish-bosheth heard that Abner was dead in Hebron, he lost heart, and all Israel was afraid.

There were two men, commanders in the army of the son of Saul. One was called Baanah and the other Rechab, the sons of Rimmon of Beeroth of the tribe of Benjamin—for Beeroth was counted as part of Benjamin, until the Beerothites fled to Gittaim where they live as strangers to this day.

Now Saul's son Jonathan had a son with two lame feet. When he was five years old, the news of Saul and Jonathan had come from Jezreel. His nurse had picked him up and fled, and in the haste of flight he had fallen and was crippled from that day on. His name was Mephibosheth. Rechab and Baanah, the sons of Rimmon of Beeroth, came to Ish-bosheth's house in the heat of midday as he lay sleeping on his bed. And look, here sat the woman cleaning wheat at the door of the house and she had fallen fast asleep, and Rechab and his brother Baanah slipped into the house and into his bedroom and there lay Ish-bosheth on his bed, and they stabbed him and killed him and cut off his head and took his head, and walked all night through the Valley of the Jordan and brought Ish-bosheth's head to David in Hebron and said, Here you are! This is the head of Ish-bosheth son of Saul, your enemy, who wanted to take your life. Today the Lord has avenged my lord the king upon Saul and his seed! David answered, By the life of the Lord who has delivered me out of every adversity, didn't I seize and kill the fellow in Ziklag who told me Saul was dead and thought he brought good news and looked for his reward? These wicked men have killed an innocent man in his house in his bed! How much the more will I demand his blood at your hands and wipe you off the face of the earth! And David ordered his young men to kill them, and he cut off their hands and feet and hung them over the pond at

Hebron. But Ish-bosheth's head they took and buried in Abner's grave at Hebron.

■ ■ ■

AND all the tribes of Israel came to David in Hebron and said, Look, we are your blood and bone. Even before, when Saul was our king, it was you who led Israel into battle and home again. It was you to whom the Lord spoke, and said, You shall shepherd My people Israel and become ruler of Israel. And all the elders of Israel came to the king, and King David made a covenant with them before the Lord in Hebron and they anointed David king of Israel. David was thirty years old when he became king, and he reigned forty years. In Hebron he reigned over Judah for seven years and six months, and in Jerusalem he reigned thirty-three years over all Israel and Judah.

And now the king and his men marched upon Jerusalem, against the Jebusites who lived there. The Jebusites said to David, You'll never get in here! But David captured the stronghold of Zion, which is the City of David.

*On that day David said, The first one to climb the ramparts and slay these lame and these blind whom my soul loathes shall be my chief and my commander. And Joab, the son of Zeruiah, was first to climb in and he became commander. And that's why they say, Don't let the blind or the lame into the house of the Lord.

And David lived in the stronghold and

---

* The meaning of II Sam. 5:9 is obscure. We interpolate I Chron. 11:6.

named it the City of David, and around it he built a city from Millo in toward the center. And David grew more and more powerful, for the Lord, God of hosts, was with him. Hiram, king of Tyre, sent envoys to David, and cedarwood, and carpenters, and stonemasons to build him a palace. And David understood that the Lord had confirmed him as king over Israel and exalted his kingship for the sake of His people Israel. After David left Hebron, he took still more wives and concubines in Jerusalem and more sons and more daughters were born to David. These are the names of the children who were born to him in Jerusalem: Shammua, Shobab, Nathan, and Solomon, Ibhar, Elishua, Nepheg, and Japhia, Elishama, Eliada, and Eliphelet.

When the Philistines heard that David had been anointed king of Israel, they came in full force to conquer David. As soon as David heard, he moved down into the stronghold. But the Philistines came and spread across the Valley of Rephaim. And David asked the Lord, Shall I go up and fight the Philistines? Will You deliver them into my hand? The Lord said, Go up and I will deliver the Philistines into your hand. And David came to Baal-perazim and defeated them and said, The Lord has broken through my enemies for me like a breaking floodwater. And he called the place Baal-perazim, meaning, the Lord breaks through. And the Philistines had left their idols behind, and David and his men carried them off.

But the Philistines returned and again they spread across the Valley of Rephaim. David came to the Lord and asked the Lord, who said, Don't go up. Go around and take them from behind the thorn trees. When you hear a rustling move through the tops of the thorn trees, fall upon them, for it is the Lord moving ahead to attack the army of the Philistines. And David did as the Lord commanded him and routed the Philistines from Geba all the way to Gezer.

. .

ONCE again David gathered the pick of the young men of Israel—an army of thirty thousand—and they set out from Kiriath-jearim in Judah to bring away the ark of God, which is called by the name of the Lord of hosts upon the throne of cherubim. They carried the ark of God out of the house of Abinadab, who lived on the hill, and they set it on a new cart, and his sons Uzzah and Ahio went down the hill with the new cart. Uzzah walked alongside and Ahio walked ahead, and David and all the house of Israel danced with all their might and rejoiced before the Lord and sang to the lyres and lutes, the timbrels and the cymbals and the harps. And as they passed the threshing floor of Nacon, the oxen stumbled and Uzzah reached for the ark of God to steady it, and the Lord's anger broke out against Uzzah because he had reached his hand for the ark, and he died there, beside the ark of God. And David was angry because the Lord had broken out against Uzzah and had broken him in the place which is called Perez-uzzah and means the breaking of Uzzah to this day. On that day David was afraid of the Lord and said to himself, Shall I let the ark of the Lord come to me? He didn't want to take the ark of the Lord with him into the City of David and had them turn

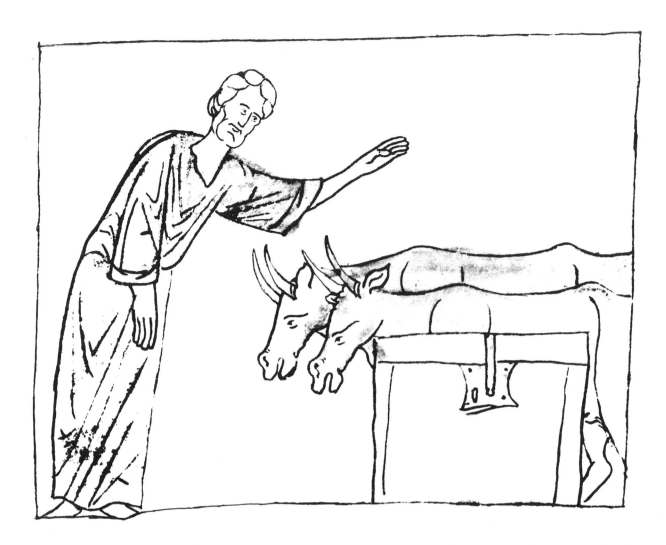

aside and take it to the house of Obed-edom, the Gittite.

The ark of the Lord remained in the House of Obed-edom the Gittite for three months, and the Lord blessed Obed-edom and all his house. When they told King David how the Lord blessed Obed-edom and his whole house and everything that belonged to him for the sake of the ark of God, he went down and brought the ark of God out of Obed-edom's house into the City of David. And they rejoiced, and every time the bearers moved the ark of the Lord six steps forward, they stopped and sacrificed an ox and a fatted lamb. And

David, dressed in a priestly linen ephod, danced with all his might and whirled before the Lord. And David and all the house of Israel carried up the ark of the Lord and shouted and blew the horn.

And as the ark of the Lord entered the City of David, Michal daughter of Saul looked out of the window and saw King David leaping and dancing and whirling before the Lord, and she despised him in her heart. They brought the ark of the Lord into the city and set it in its place in the middle of the tent David had put up for it. David offered burnt offerings to the Lord, and peace offerings, and when he had finished offering the burnt offerings and the peace offerings, he blessed the people in the name of the Lord of hosts and gave out to all the people, to that whole multitude of Israel—every man and every woman—a loaf of bread, a large piece of the meat, and a raisin cake, and then the people went home, each to his own house. When David went home to bless his household, Saul's daughter Michal came out to meet him and said, The king of Israel did himself proud today exposing himself before the eyes of his own servants' slave women like any low-life. David said, I shall be a dancer before the

Lord who has chosen me over your father and all his house and made me ruler over His people Israel! I will lower myself and make myself even smaller in my own eyes, and yet be honored among these very slave women of whom you speak! And Saul's daughter Michal bore no children to her dying day.

..

Now the king sat in his palace and the Lord gave him rest from his enemies all around him, and he said to the prophet Nathan, Look how I dwell here in a cedar

palace while the ark of God dwells under a cloth tent! Nathan said, Do what your heart tells you, because the Lord is with you. But that night it happened—it happened that the word of the Lord came to Nathan, saying, Go to my servant David and say, This is what the Lord has said: Should you build Me a house for Me to dwell in? I have not dwelled in a house from the day I brought the children of Israel up out of Egypt to this day, but have traveled about in a tent and a tabernacle. Have I ever, in all the time that I traveled everywhere with the children of Israel, spoken to any of Israel's leaders whom I appointed to shepherd My people Israel and said, Why haven't you built Me a cedar house? Therefore go to My servant David and say, This is what the Lord of hosts has said: I took you out of the pasture where you followed behind the flock to lead My people Israel! I have been with you wherever you have gone and cut down the enemies out of your path, and I shall make you a name as great as any name on the earth. I shall make a place for My people Israel and shall plant them in it, to live in it and never be afraid again. The children of malice shall not oppress them as they used to do in the old days when I appointed leaders over My people Israel. I shall give you rest from all your enemies. The Lord proclaims that it is He, the Lord, who will build a house for you. And when your days are done and you sleep with your fathers, I shall raise up an offspring out of your body and I will establish his kingship. He shall build a house for My Name, and I will establish the throne of his kingship forever. I shall be a father to

him and he shall be a son to Me. When he does wrong, I shall punish him with the rod the way men beat their children, but I shall never withdraw my love from him as I withdrew it from Saul, whom I removed out of your way. For your house and your kingdom shall endure in My care and your throne shall endure forever.

When Nathan had told David these words and this vision, King David went in and sat down before the Lord and said, Who am I, my Lord God, and what is my house that You have brought me so far? And now even this seems too little to You, my Lord God, for You promise Your servant's house things to come, far in the future, which is beyond the sight of man, my Lord God. What else is there that David can say to You? You know Your servant, my Lord God! For Your word's sake and from Your heart have You done all these great things and revealed them to Your servant, whereby You grow in greatness, Lord God! For there is no one like You, and no God except You according to everything our ears have heard! Where is there another nation upon earth like Your people Israel, whom God has redeemed to be His people, and to make Himself a name by His great and terrible deeds for Your land and for the sake of Your people, driving nations and their gods out of the path of Your own people, whom You redeemed for Yourself out of Egypt. You have made Your people Israel to be Your people forever, and You, Lord, became their God. Now, Lord God, make forever true the word that You have spoken about Your servant, and to his house, and do as You have said! Then Your Name shall be great forever and men will say, The Lord of hosts is God of Israel, and the house of Your servant David will stand in Your care forever. It is because You, O Lord of hosts, God of Israel, have spoken in Your servant's ear and said, I will build you a house, that Your servant has taken heart and prayed this prayer to You. Now, my Lord God, You are God and Your words will be true and You have said these good things to Your servant, so begin even now to bless Your servant's house so that it will stand in Your care forever, for You my Lord God have spoken it. May Your servant's house be forever blessed with Your blessing.

■ ■

AND after this it happened that David beat the Philistines and subdued them, and took Metheg-ammah out of the hand of the Philistines. And the Moabites, too, he defeated and made them lie on the ground and measured them with a cord; he measured off two cords' lengths of them and that many he put to death, and one full cord's length and that many he let live, and the Moabites became David's vassals and paid him tribute. And David defeated Hadadezer son of Rehob, king of Zobah, who was on his way to the river Euphrates to restore his dominion. David captured one thousand seven hundred of his horsemen and twenty thousand foot soldiers and lamed all but one hundred of their horses, which he kept for himself. When the Arameans of Damascus came to the aid of Hadadezer, king of Zobah, David struck down two-and-twenty thousand of their men. He set up garrisons in Aram Damascus, and the Arameans became David's vassals and paid him tribute, for the Lord gave David victory wherever he went. David took the golden shields Hadadezer's men wore and brought them to Jerusalem, and from Betah and Berothai, the cities of Hadadezer, King David took a very great deal of copper. When Toi, king of Hamath, heard that David had defeated the forces of Hadadezer, he sent his son Joram to greet King David and to bless him because he had fought and defeated Hadadezer—for Toi too was at war with Hadadezer—and Joram brought with him objects of silver and gold and copper. King David sanctified them to the Lord together with the silver and gold of all the nations he had subdued, from Edom, from Moab, from the Ammonites, from the Philistines, from Amalek, and the spoils he had taken from Hadadezer son of Rehob, king of Zobah. And David made a name for himself. When he returned from his defeat of Edom in the Valley of Salt— eighteen thousand men—he set up garrisons throughout Edom and all the Edomites became King David's vassals, for the Lord helped David wherever he went.

And David was king of all Israel and brought law and justice to all his people. Joab son of Zeruiah was in command of the army; Jehoshaphat son of Ahilud was recorder; Zadok son of Ahitub and Ahimelech son of Abiathar were priests, and Seraiah was the scribe. Benaiah son of Jehoiada was in charge of the Cherethites and the Pelethites. And David's sons served as priests.

AND David said, Is there anyone left of the house of Saul to whom I may show friendship for Jonathan's sake? There was a servant of the house of Saul whose name was Ziba. They summoned him before David and King David said, Are you Ziba? He said, I am your servant. The king said, Is there anyone at all left of the house of Saul to whom I may show friendship and fulfill the oath I swore to Jonathan before the Lord? Ziba said, There is still a son of Jonathan, and his feet are lame. The king asked, Where is he? Ziba said, Well, he lives in the house of Machir, son of Ammiel, in Lo-debar. And so King David had him brought from the house of Machir, son of Ammiel.

Mephibosheth son of Jonathan, the son of Saul, came before King David and bowed down with his face to the ground and prostrated himself, but David said, Mephibosheth! He said, Here is your servant. I am your slave. David said, Don't be afraid, for I will be your friend for your father Jonathan's sake. I will restore to you all your grandfather Saul's inheritance, and you yourself shall eat at my table every day. Again Mephibosheth fell to the ground and said, What is your servant that you should notice a dead dog like me? The king called Saul's servant Ziba and said, Whatever belonged to Saul and to his whole household I give to your lord's son. Work his land, you and your sons and your servants, and bring in the harvest to feed your lord's household, but as for your lord's son, Mephibosheth, he shall eat at my table every day. And Ziba had fifteen sons and twenty servants. Ziba said, Your servant will do whatever my lord the king commands his servant. And Mephibosheth, said the king, shall eat at my table as if he were one of the king's sons. Mephibosheth had a little son called Mica. And Ziba and all his household served Mephibosheth. But Mephibosheth lived in Jerusalem and ate at the king's table every day. And he was lame in both his feet.

AND after this it happened that the king of the Ammonites died, and his son Hanun became king in his stead. David said, I will be a friend to Hanun son of Nahash in return for the friendship his father showed me. And David sent his envoys to console him about his father. Now when David's envoys came to the land of the Ammonites, the princes of Ammon said to their lord Hanun, You think David means to honor your father when he sends you these consolers? Don't you think he sent his envoys to spy out the city, and search it out, and destroy it? And Hanun seized David's envoys and shaved off half their beards and cut their skirts in half up to their buttocks and sent them on their way. When they told David, he sent messengers to meet them because they had been very much shamed. The king sent word to say, Stay in Jericho till your beards have grown. Then you can come home.

The Ammonites saw they were in bad odor with David, and they sent to hire twenty thousand foot soldiers from the

Arameans of Beth-rehob and the Arameans of Zobah, and a thousand men from the king of Maacah and twelve thousand men from Tob. When David heard, he sent Joab with the whole army of warriors. And the Ammonites marched out and drew themselves up for battle at the entrance of the city, but the Arameans of Zobah and Rehob and the men of Tob and Maacah stayed in the open field. Joab saw he was under attack from the front and the back and he chose a small troop of the choicest young men of Israel and ranged himself against the Arameans. The rest of the army he put under the command of his brother Abishai to range them against the Ammonites. He said, If the Arameans are too strong for me, you will come to my help; if the Ammonites are too strong for you, then I will come and help you. Take heart and be strong for the sake of our people and the cities of our God! The Lord will do as He pleases. And Joab and his men marched against the Arameans, and they fled before him. When the Ammonites saw the Arameans in flight, they fled from Abishai into the city. And Joab stopped fighting the Ammonites and came to Jerusalem. The Arameans saw that Israel had routed them and regrouped. Hadadezer sent across the river for the Arameans, and they came to Helam with Shobach, the commander of Hadadezer's army, at their head. When they told David, he gathered the forces of Israel, crossed the Jordan, and came to Helam. The Arameans drew themselves up for battle against David and fought with him, and Israel put them to flight. David killed seven hundred Aramean charioteers and forty thousand horsemen and struck down Shobach, the commander of their army, so that he died there. When all the vassal kings under Hadadezer saw that they had been defeated by Israel, they made peace with Israel and became its vassals. From that day on, the Arameans were afraid to help the Ammonites.

· ·

WHEN the year had turned, in the season when kings march into battle, David sent Joab and his soldiers and all Israel to destroy the Ammonites and besiege the city of Rabbah. But David remained in Jerusalem. Now it happened one evening that David rose from his bed and was walking to and fro on the roof of the royal palace, and from the roof he saw a woman bathing, and the woman was very beautiful.

He inquired about the woman. Someone said, Isn't that Bathsheba daughter of Eliam, the wife of Uriah the Hittite? David sent messengers to fetch her, and she came to him and he made love to her, for she had just purified herself from her unclean-

ness. Then she went back to her house, and the woman was with child and sent word to tell David, I am with child.

David sent word to Joab: Send me Uriah the Hittite. And Joab sent Uriah to David. Uriah came, and David asked him how Joab was, how was the army, and how was the war going. Then David said, Go down to your house and bathe your feet, and Uriah left the royal palace followed by a present of meat from the king's table. But Uriah slept at the entrance of the royal palace with his lord's soldiers. He didn't go down to his house. When they told David, Uriah didn't go down to his house,

David said to him, You've come a long way! Why didn't you go down to your house? Uriah said, The ark and the armies of Israel and Judah are living in tents, and my lord Joab and my lord's soldiers camp out in the open field. How can I go home to my house and eat and drink and lie with my wife? As you live and as the Lord lives, how could I do that? So David said, Stay another day and tomorrow I'll send you back. Uriah stayed the day in Jerusalem and on the next day David invited him to eat and drink with him and got Uriah drunk, and in the evening, when Uriah left, he lay down to sleep with the king's

soldiers and didn't go down to his house.

In the morning David wrote Joab a letter and sent it with Uriah. In the letter he wrote, Put Uriah in the front lines where the fighting is heaviest, and you withdraw so that he'll get hit and be killed. And Joab surrounded the city and put Uriah where he knew the fighters were most warlike. And they came out of the city to fight Joab and some of the officers of David's army fell and Uriah the Hittite died too. And Joab sent David a full account of the battle and commanded the messenger to say: When you have finished telling the king everything that happened in the battle and you see the king is getting angry and says, Why did you fight so close to the

city? Didn't you know they would shoot down from the wall? Don't you remember how Abimelech son of Jerubbesheth was killed? Didn't a woman roll a millstone down from the wall on him and he died in Thebez? Why did you fight so close to the wall? Then you must say, Your servant Uriah the Hittite is dead too.

The messenger set out and came to the king and told him everything Joab had sent him to say: Their men outnumbered us and came out against us into the open field, and we fought them back to the gate of the city, but the archers shot down from the wall on your servants and killed some eighteen of my lord's men and your servant Uriah the Hittite is dead too. David

said, Here's what you must say to Joab: Don't feel bad about this. The sword devours now this man, now that. Keep up the attack on the city and destroy it! Encourage him.

When Uriah's wife heard that her husband Uriah was dead, she lamented him. As soon as her mourning was over, David sent for her and brought her to the palace, and she became his wife and bore him a son.

But David had done evil in the Lord's eyes.

The Lord sent the prophet Nathan to David, and he came to him and said, There were two men in the same city. One was rich, and one was poor. The rich man had a great many sheep and oxen, but the poor man had only one little ewe lamb he had bought and nursed, and it grew up with him like one of his children and shared his bite of bread and drank out of his cup and lay in his lap and was like a daughter to him. There came a visitor to the rich man, but it seemed to him a pity to take one of his own sheep or cattle to prepare for the visitor who had come to him, and so he took the poor man's lamb and prepared it for the man who had come to visit him. David's anger flared against the man and he said, As the Lord lives, the man who did this deserves to die even if he pays four times the value of the lamb, because he had no pity.

Nathan said, You are the man! Hear the word of the Lord, God of Israel, who says,

It was I who anointed you king of Israel, and I who saved you out of the hand of Saul and gave you your lord's house and put your lord's wives in your lap and gave you the house of Israel and Judah, and if that is not enough I will give you this and that on top of it. Why did you scorn the Lord's word and do this evil in His sight? You have slain Uriah the Hittite with the sword and taken his wife to be your wife; with the sword of the Ammonite have you murdered him! Now the sword shall never leave your house, for you have scorned Me and taken Uriah the Hittite's wife to be your wife! This is what the Lord says to you: Know that I shall raise up evil against you out of your own house and I shall take your wives in front of your eyes and give them to your neighbor and he will lie with them in the eye of this sun. Yes! You did it in secret, but I shall do the thing in front of all Israel, in the sun! David said, I have sinned against the Lord! And Nathan said, The Lord has taken your sin away; you shall not die. But because your deed has given occasion to the mouths of the enemies of the people of the Lord, the son who will be born to you will die and be dead. Then Nathan went home.

And the Lord afflicted the child that Uriah's wife had borne David, and it became deathly ill. And David begged God for the young child and fasted and came home and slept all night on the floor. The elders of his household tried to raise him from the floor, but he would not rise, and would not eat with them. On the seventh day the child died. David's servants were afraid to tell him that the child was dead and said, He would not listen to us when the child was alive, how can we tell him the child is dead? He might do himself harm. David saw his servants whispering and knew the child was dead and said, Is the child dead? They said, He is dead. And David got up from the floor, bathed and anointed himself and changed his clothes, and went into the house of the Lord and prostrated himself. Then he went home and asked for food and they put it before him and he ate. His servants said, What are you doing? While the child was alive you fasted and wept and now that he is dead you get up and you eat! He said, While the child was alive, I fasted and wept because I thought, Who knows! The Lord might have pity on me and let the child live. Why should I fast now that he is dead? Can I bring him back again? I will go to him, but he will never come back to me! And David consoled his wife Bathsheba and went in and lay with her, and she bore a son and he called him Solomon, and the Lord loved him and sent the prophet Nathan to name him Jedidiah by the grace of the Lord.

And Joab fought against Ammonite Rabbah and captured the royal city and sent messengers to David saying, I have fought against Rabbah and taken the city of waters. Call up the rest of the army, surround the city and take it yourself. If I take it, it will be called by my name. And David called up the whole army and marched against Rabbah and fought and captured it. He took the crown off their king's head and it weighed a talent of gold and was set with precious stones, and it was put on David's head. He brought a large booty out of the city, and brought out the people who lived in it and put them to work with saws and iron picks and iron axes and set them to make bricks, as he did with all the Ammonite cities. Then David and all the army returned to Jerusalem.

∙∙

THIS is what happened afterward: David's son Absalom had a beautiful sister called Tamar. By another of his wives David had a son Amnon, and Amnon fell in love with Tamar. He was so unhappy that he grew sick with longing for his sister Tamar, because she was a virgin and it did not seem possible to Amnon to do anything to her. Now Amnon had a friend, Jonadab, the son of David's brother Shimeah. Jonadab was a very clever man. He said, You're getting thinner by the day, my prince. Tell me why. Amnon said, I love Tamar, my

brother Absalom's sister! Jonadab said, Lie down in your bed as if you were ill. When your father comes to see you, you must say, Why don't you let my sister Tamar come and feed me some food and cook it where I can watch her? I'll take it from her hands and eat it. So Amnon lay down as if he were ill, and when the king came to see him, Amnon said, Why don't you let my sister Tamar come and make me some cakes where I can watch her and I'll eat them from her hand? David sent word to Tamar in the palace and said, Go to your brother Amnon's house and cook him some dish to make him better. Tamar went to her brother Amnon's house and he was lying in his bed. She took dough and kneaded it and made cakes where he could watch her, and she baked them, and took them out of the pan, and served him, but he refused to eat and said, Everybody leave

the room! When everybody had left, Amnon said, Bring the cakes you have made me into my room and I'll take them from your hands and eat them. And Tamar took the cakes that she had made him and brought them to her brother Amnon in his room and served him, and he took hold of Tamar and said, Come, sister, and lie here with me! But she said, Don't do it, my brother! Don't force me! We don't do such things in Israel! Don't do this abominable thing! And I! Where would I go in my shame? And you'll be one of Israel's scoundrels. Talk to the king! He won't refuse to give me to you! But Amnon would not listen to her and overpowered her and took her by force and lay with her. And now Amnon felt a very great loathing for her and hated her with a hatred greater than the love with which he had loved her, and Amnon said, Get up, and get out of here! She said, That you send me away is a greater wrong than the other that you have done to me! But he would not listen to her, called his servant, and said, Get this woman away from me. Put her out in the street and lock the door behind her! And his servant put her out and locked the door behind her. And she was wearing the tunic of many colors that the king's daughters wear as long as they are virgins and Tamar took dust and put it on her head and tore her tunic of many colors and put her hands on her head and walked away crying out loud. Her brother Absalom said to her, Has your brother Amnon been with you? Be quiet for now, my sister; he is your brother! Don't take it so to heart. And so Tamar remained desolate, in the house of her brother Absalom.

King David was very angry when he heard about it, but he did not punish Amnon, whom he loved because he was his firstborn. As for Absalom, he said nothing at all to Amnon either good or ill, for Absalom hated Amnon because he had violated his sister Tamar.

It happened two years later that Absalom had his sheepshearing in Baal-hazor, near Ephraim, and Absalom invited all the king's sons to the feast. He went to the king and said, Look, your servant has a sheepshearing. Won't you, my king and your court, go with your servant? The king said, No, my son, we can't all go with you. We'd be a burden to you. And although Absalom urged him, he would not go and dismissed him with his blessing. But Absalom said, Why don't you let my brother Amnon go with us? The king said, Why should he go with you? Absalom pressed him and so the king let Amnon and all the king's sons go with Absalom, and Absalom prepared a feast fit for a king. And Absalom instructed his servants and said, Keep your eye on Amnon and when he is in good spirits from the wine, and I say to you, Strike Amnon down, then you

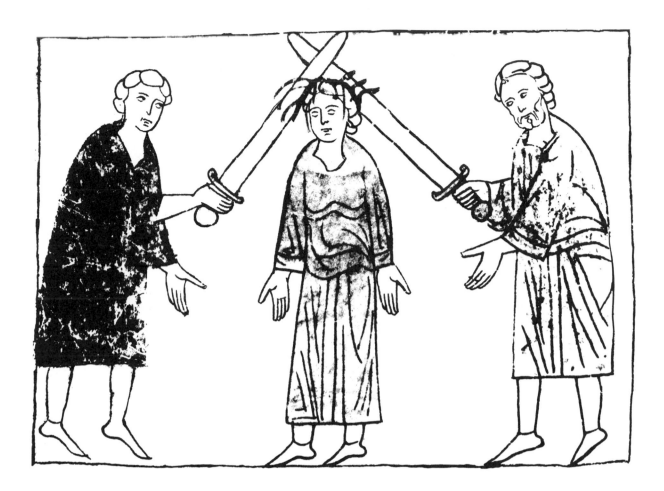

shall kill him. Don't be afraid, because I have commanded you to do it. Be strong and go to it bravely. And Absalom's servants did what he had commanded them. The king's sons all jumped up, mounted their mules, and fled.

They were still on the road when the rumor reached David that Absalom had slain every one of the king's sons and that not one of them was left alive. The king rose and tore his clothes and lay down on the ground, and his servants, who stood all around him, tore their clothes. But Jonadab, the son of David's brother Shimeah, said, My lord king mustn't think that all the young princes have been killed. Only Amnon is dead, because this is what

Absalom has had in mind since the day his brother violated his sister Tamar. My lord king mustn't think that all the king's sons are dead, because it's only Amnon. And the young man on watch raised his eyes, and look, here came a great crowd of people down the mountain road from Horon. Jonadab said, Here come the princes, just as your servant has said. And as he finished speaking, look! here came the princes weeping aloud, and the king and all the court wept very bitterly. But Absalom fled to Talmai son of Ammihud, king of Geshur. And David mourned his son, day in day out.

Absalom had fled and gone to Geshur, and stayed there for three years. And the king's soul longed for Absalom, for he had consoled himself about Amnon's death.

▪ ▪

JOAB son of Zeruiah saw how the king's soul longed for Absalom. And he sent to Tekoa and had them bring back a wise woman and said to her, Dress yourself as if you were in mourning; don't anoint yourself with oil. Act like a woman who has mourned her dead a long time. Go to the king and say what I will tell you. And Joab put the words into her mouth.

The woman of Tekoa came and fell face-down before the king and prostrated herself and said, Help me, O king! The king said, What is it? The woman said, I'm a widow and my husband is dead. Your maidservant had two sons and they quarreled out in the field, and because there was no one to intervene between them, one of them struck the other and killed him. And look, now the whole family has risen up against your servant. They say, Hand over this killer of his brother and we will put him to death for the life of his brother whom he has killed. They want to take my only heir, and quench my last ember so that there will be no name nor remnant of my husband left on the face of the earth. Go home, said the king, and I will render my judgment in your case. And the woman of Tekoa said, Let the guilt be upon me and my father's house. My lord the king and my lord the king's throne shall be guiltless. The king said, If anyone says anything against you, bring him before me, and he won't trouble you again. She said, In the name of the Lord your

God may my lord the king prevent him who would avenge the blood of the dead with more destruction and kill my other son as well. And he said, As the Lord God lives, no one shall touch a hair of your son's head. The woman said, Permit your maidservant to say something to my lord the king. Say it, said the king.

The woman said, Isn't this the same sin against the people of the Lord of which the king is guilty when he will not bring home his banished son? We all die! We're like water spilled on the ground that can never be gathered up. God will not give your son his life again. Why does it seem right to you to keep your banished son banished from him? I came to speak to my lord the king because these people frighten me. Your servant thought to herself, I will speak with the king. Perhaps the king will do what his maidservant says! The king will listen to his maidservant and save me from the hand of those who wish to destroy both me and my son and cut us out of God's inheritance. Your maidservant thought, The word of my lord the king will be a consolation because my lord the king is like an angel of God who can distinguish good from evil, and may the Lord your God be with you.

Now the king said to the woman, I'll ask you a question; don't keep anything from me. The woman said, Let my lord the king ask. The king said, Does Joab have a hand in this? The woman answered, By your life, my lord and king, there's no turning right or left or getting away from what my lord the king has said. Yes, it was your servant Joab who commanded me and put these words into your maidservant's mouth! It was to show the matter in another light that your servant Joab devised this plan, but my lord has the wisdom of an angel of God and knows everything that happens on this earth. The king said to Joab, Look, I'll do what you say. Go and bring young Absalom back. And Joab fell with his face to the ground and prostrated himself and blessed the king and said, Now your servant knows I have found favor in the eyes of my lord the king because the king does what his servant has asked. Joab set off for Geshur and brought Absalom back to Jerusalem, but the king said, Let him go back to his own house, he shall not see my face. And so Absalom came back to his own house, but did not see the king's face.

As for Absalom, there was no man in all of Israel so admired for his beauty. From the sole of his foot to the crown of his head he was flawless. When his hair was cut—which happened every year, when it became too heavy for him—it weighed two hundred measures according to the royal standard. Absalom had three sons and a daughter called Tamar, and she was a beautiful girl.

And Absalom lived two years in Jerusalem and did not see the king's face. And so he sent for Joab in order to send him to the king, but Joab didn't want to come to him. He sent for him a second time, but he still didn't want to come. Now Absalom said to his servants, You see that field of Joab's next to mine—where he grows his barley? Go, set it on fire. And so Absalom's servants set the field on fire. Joab got up and went to Absalom's house and said, Why have your servants set my

field on fire? Absalom said, Look, I sent to you to say, Come here so that I can send you to the king to say, Your son Absalom says, Why did I leave Geshur? It would be better for me if I had stayed there! Now let me see the king's face, and if there's any guilt in me, let him put me to death. Joab went in to the king and told him, and the king summoned Absalom, and Absalom went to the king and prostrated himself before the king with his face to the ground, and the king kissed Absalom.

• •

THERE came a time when Absalom got himself a chariot and horses and fifty men to run in front of him. He'd get up early in the morning and stand in the road outside the city gate. If anybody came along with some matter of justice to bring before the king for judgment, Absalom would call him over and say, What town do you come from?—The man would say, Your servant is from such and such a tribe of Israel. Then Absalom would say, Look, your case is right and just, but none of the king's people are going to listen. And he would say, If only they would make me a judge in this country, then anyone who had a case or a dispute could come to me, and I'd see justice done! Or if someone approached to prostrate himself before Absalom, Absalom would reach out his hand and take him and kiss him. That's how Absalom behaved to all the Israelites who came to the king for judgment. That is how he stole the hearts of the people of Israel.

Four years went by and Absalom came to the king and said, Let me go to Hebron and fulfill the vow I vowed the Lord. When I sat in Geshur, your servant vowed a vow. I said, If the Lord will bring me back to Jerusalem, I shall worship the Lord in Hebron. The king said, Go in peace, and he set out for Hebron. But Absalom had sent his spies to all the tribes of Israel. They said, When you hear the sound of the trumpet you must say Absalom has become king in Hebron! But there went with Absalom two hundred men from Jerusalem who had been invited along, and went meaning no harm and knowing nothing of the matter. And Absalom summoned Ahithophel the Gilonite, David's counselor, from the city of Giloh, where he was offering sacrifices, and the conspiracy grew in strength and more and more people joined Absalom.

There came a messenger and told David, Israel's heart has turned to Absalom! David spoke to his court in Jerusalem and said, Let us up and flee! There'll be no escaping Absalom here. Hurry, so he won't catch up with us and capture us and bring down disaster upon us and put the city to the sword! The king's people said, The king must do whatever he thinks best. Look, we are your servants! And so the king left the city, with his whole household following behind, except for ten concubines whom he left behind to take care of the palace.

And the king and all his household marched out of the city and halted by the last house, and the servants of his court stayed at his side, but all the Cherethites and all the Pelethites and all the Gittites—the six hundred men who had followed him from Gath—marched past the king. The king said to Ittai the Gittite, Why are you coming with us too? Go back and stay with the new king, for you are a stranger; you too are an exile from your own land. It was only yesterday that you came, and today I should make you wander who knows where with us? I must go where I can. Turn back and take your kin with you, and may the Lord's mercy and truth be with you! But Ittai answered, As the Lord lives and as my lord the king lives, wherever my lord the king will be, whether to live or die, that's where your servant will be too. The king said, Well, then go with me. And so Ittai the Gittite, and all his men and all his household of women and children passed by.

And the whole land wept aloud when the army marched past. And the king passed over the Kidron Valley, and all the army continued on the way that leads into the wilderness. And look! here came Zadok and Abiathar and all the Levites carrying the ark of the covenant of God, and they set the ark of the covenant of God down until the whole army had passed out of the city. But the king said to Zadok, Take the ark of God back to the city. If the Lord is merciful He will bring me back and show it to me in its rightful place in Jerusalem. But if He says, I have no delight in you, here I am! Let Him do with me whatever He likes. And the king said to Zadok the priest, Look, go back to the city in peace, you and Abiathar, and your son Ahimaaz and Abiathar's son Jonathan. Look, I'll be sitting in the wilderness waiting for news from you. And so Zadok and

Abiathar took the ark of God back to Jerusalem and they remained there, but David went up the Mount of Olives barefoot with his head covered, weeping as he went, and all who were with him covered their heads and wept as they went. When they told David that Ahithophel, his chief counselor, was in league with Absalom, he said, Lord, turn Ahithophel's counsel into foolishness!

And as David came to the top of the mountain, where one worships God, Hushai the Archite came to meet the king with his clothes torn and dirt on his head, and David said, If you come with me, you'll be a burden to me, but if you go back to the city and say to Absalom, I will be my lord's servant as I have been your father's servant before you—then you can frustrate Ahithophel's counsel for me. Zadok and Abiathar, the priests, are with you. Whatever you will hear in the king's palace, tell it to the priests Zadok and Abiathar. Look, their two sons are with them—Zadok's son Ahimaaz, and Abiathar's son Jonathan. Through them you can pass on to me everything you hear. And so David's friend Hushai came to Jerusalem as Absalom was entering the city.

When David had come a short way down from the top of the mountain, look, here came Ziba, Mephibosheth's servant, toward him with a pair of saddled asses laden with two hundred loaves of bread, a hundred raisin cakes, a hundred baskets of fresh fruits, and a skin of wine. The king asked Ziba, What are you doing with these things? Ziba said, The asses are for the king's household to ride on, the bread and fruits are for the young men to eat, and the wine is for those who grow faint in the wilderness to drink. The king said, And where is your lord's son? Ziba said, Well, he stayed in Jerusalem because he thinks, This is the day on which the house of Israel will restore me my father's kingdom. The king said, Well, then, everything that belongs to Mephibosheth shall be yours. Ziba said, I bow myself down before my lord the king and may I always have your good favor.

When King David got to Bahurim, look, there came out a man of Saul's family. The man's name was Shimei son of Gera, and he came out cursing and throwing stones at David and at the servants of his court even though the king's soldiers and warriors surrounded him right and left. Shimei cursed him and shouted, Out! Get out, you bloodthirsty lout! The Lord has repaid you for the blood of the house of Saul in whose place you have become king! Now the Lord has put the kingdom in the hands of your son Absalom and you're stuck in your misery, because you're a man of blood! Abishai son of Zeruiah said, Why is this dead dog allowed to curse my lord the king? Let me go over and knock off his head! But the king said, You sons of Zeruiah—What do you and I have to do with one another? Let him curse! It was the Lord who told him, Curse David! Who's to question why he does it? And to Abishai and to all the servants of his court David said, Look, my own flesh and blood wants me dead, so why not this Benjaminite? Let him curse in peace, for the Lord has told him to. Perhaps the Lord will see my misery and repay me today's curses with good to come. And David and his people walked on with Shimei walking beside them along the side of the hill, walking and cursing and throwing stones at him and clumps of dirt.

And so the king and his people arrived at the Jordan tired out and there they rested. But Absalom and all the people, and all the men of Israel entered Jerusalem, and Ahithophel was with them. When David's friend Hushai the Archite entered Absalom's presence, he cried, Long live the king! Long live the king! Absalom said, Is this your love for your friend David? Why haven't you gone with your friend? No, said Hushai, I belong with him whom the Lord and the people, and all Israel, have chosen, and with him will I remain! Besides, whom should I serve if not David's son? As I have served your father, so I will now serve you!

And Absalom asked Ahithophel, Give us your counsel: what shall we do? Ahithophel said, Go in to your father's concubines whom he has left behind to take care of the palace, and then all Israel will hear that you're in bad odor with your father and it will strengthen the hand of everybody on your side. So they pitched a tent for Absalom on the roof, and Absalom went in to his father's concubines before the eyes of the whole of Israel. For if, in those days, Ahithophel gave advice, it was as if one had asked God Himself— that is how both David and Absalom depended on Ahithophel's counsel. And Ahithophel said, Let me choose twelve thousand men and I will go and chase after David tonight and fall upon him while he's tired and distraught. If I surprise them, his army will flee and I can kill only the

king and bring the whole army back to you like a bride returning to her husband. All you want is the life of the one man. Let the people live in peace.

Absalom and all the elders of Israel liked his counsel, but Absalom said, Let's call Hushai the Archite and hear what he has to say. Hushai came in and Absalom said, Ahithophel has said thus and so. Tell us, should we do what he says or not? Hushai said, It's bad advice that Ahithophel has given you this time. And he said, You know your father and his people—that they're brave and as angry as a mother bear robbed of her young. What's more, your father is a veteran soldier and won't allow his people to sleep. And, look, even now he may be hiding out in some pit or somewhere! And then if any of your soldiers happen to fall right in the beginning, a rumor might spread: the army of that fellow Absalom has been beaten! Then even the most valiant warrior with the heart of a lion will melt away because everyone in Israel knows your father is a hero and his men are brave warriors. No, I advise you to call together all Israel from Dan to Beer-sheba—as many men as the grains of sand on the seashore—and that you yourself lead them into battle. Then when we find him, in whatever place he is to be found, we'll come down upon him like the dew that falls upon the earth, so that no one, neither he nor any one of the men that are with him will be left alive! If he retreats into a city, all Israel will come with ropes and drag it down into the valley and not leave so much as a little stone. And Absalom and every man in Israel said, Hushai's advice is better than

Ahithophel's! That's how the Lord frustrated Ahithophel's good advice, because the Lord intended Absalom's destruction.

But Hushai said to the priests Zadok and Abiathar, This and this was what Ahithophel advised the elders of Israel, but I said so and so. Get word to David, quickly! Say to him, Don't stop to rest the night in the plains of the wilderness but move on, or the king and all his army will be swallowed up. Now Jonathan and Ahimaaz were waiting near a well in En-rogel, and a slave girl would come out and tell them the news, and they would go and tell King David, for they dared not let themselves be seen in the city. But a boy saw them and told Absalom, and so the two men hurried away to the house of a man in Bahurim who had a well in his yard and they climbed inside, and the woman of the house spread a cloth over the mouth of the well and poured grain over it until there was nothing to be seen. Now when Absalom's people came to the woman's house, they said, Where are Ahimaaz and Jonathan? She said, They crossed over the water. Absalom's people looked, but when they could not find them, they returned to Jerusalem. When they had gone, the two men climbed out of the well and went to find King David and said, Quick, cross the water! This and this is the counsel that Ahithophel has given against you! And David and his people rose and crossed the Jordan. Came the morning light, there was not one man left who had not crossed the Jordan.

When Ahithophel saw his counsel had not been taken, he saddled his ass, and got up and went straight home to his own city,

settled the affairs of his house, and hanged himself and died and was buried in his father's grave.

And David reached Mahanaim, but Absalom and the army of Israel crossed the Jordan. And Absalom put Amasa in charge of the army instead of Joab. Now Amasa was the son of a man called Ithra, a Jesraelite, who had lain with Abigail, the daughter of Nahash, the sister of Zeruiah, Joab's mother. And Israel and Absalom camped in Gilead.

When David arrived in Mahanaim, Shobi son of Nahash of Rabbath-ammon, and Machir son of Ammiel of Lo-debar, and Barzillai, a Gileadite from Rogelim, brought beds, bowls, and earthenware, and wheat, barley, flour, roasted grain, beans, lentils, and honey, and curds from the cows, and cheese from the sheep for David and his people to eat, for they said, The people will have grown hungry and tired and thirsty in the wilderness. And David mustered his army and set over them captains of thousands and captains of hundreds and divided the army and put one-third under the command of Joab, one-third under Joab's brother Abishai, and one third under Ittai the Gittite. And the king said to his army, I will march with you too. But they said, You mustn't march with us. If we flee, or if half of us die, nobody would notice, but you are worth ten thousand of us. You help us more by staying in the city. The king said, I will do whatever you think best. And the king went and stood at the gate, and the army marched out by hundreds and by thousands.

And the king commanded Joab, Abishai,

and Ittai and said, Don't hurt my son Absalom, for my sake!—And the whole army heard what the king commanded his officers about Absalom. The army marched into the field against Israel, and the battle took place in the forest of Ephraim. David's men routed the army of Israel. There was a great battle there on that day— twenty thousand men, and the battle spread across the whole region, and on that day the forest devoured more men than the sword. Absalom happened upon David's men. He was riding his mule, and the mule passed under the tangled branches of a great oak. His hair caught in the oak and there he hung between heaven and earth, and his mule walked away underneath him. A man who saw it came and told Joab and said, Listen! I saw Absalom hanging from an oak! Joab said, Listen, if you saw him, why didn't you knock him to the ground? I'd have given you ten silver pieces and a belt! The man said, If you had weighed out a thousand silver pieces into the palms of my hands, I would not have laid a hand on the king's son. Our own ears heard the king's command to you and Abishai and Ittai: Don't hurt my son Absalom, for my sake!—if I had done something wrong, you yourself would have sided against me, for nothing remains hidden from the king. Joab said, I can't stand here talking with you!—and he took three lances and thrust Absalom

through the heart as he hung alive from the oak, and ten young men, Joab's armsbearers, surrounded Absalom and beat him to death. Now Joab sounded the horn and the soldiers stopped chasing after Israel, for Joab ordered them to halt. They took Absalom down, threw him in a big pit in the forest, and piled a big heap of stones on top of it, and all Israel fled, each man to his tent.

Now Absalom, when he was still alive, had erected himself a monument in the Valley of the King because he said, I have no son to keep my name alive, and he called the monument by his name and it is called Absalom's Memorial to this day.

And Ahimaaz son of Zadok said, Let me run and bring the king the good news that the Lord has vindicated him against his enemies! Joab said, You're not the man to carry the news today. Some other day you may bring him the news, but not today, because the king's son is dead. And Joab called an Ethiopian and said, Go and tell the king what you have seen! The Ethiopian bowed to Joab and started running. But again Ahimaaz son of Zadok said, Come what may, Let me go too and run after the Ethiopian. Joab said, Why should you run, my son? You'll get no reward for this news. Ahimaaz said, Come what may, I'm going to run too! And so Joab said, So run. And Ahimaaz ran along the Jordan Valley and overtook the Ethiopian.

David was sitting between the two gates, and the watchman went up to the roof of the outer gate and looked up and here came a man running alone! He called down and told the king. The king said, If he's alone, his mouth brings good news! The man came nearer and the watchman saw a sec-

ond man running and called down to the gate, Look, here comes another man running alone! The king said, He brings good news too. The watchman on the wall said, The one in front runs like Ahimaaz son of Zadok. The king said, He's a brave fellow and brings good news! And Ahimaaz called out to the king and said, Peace! and then he prostrated himself before the king and said, Praise to the Lord, your God, who has wiped off the face of the earth those who have raised their hands against my lord the king! The king said, And is young Absalom all right? Ahimaaz said, I saw a great commotion as the king's servant Joab was sending your servant off, but I don't know what it was. The king said, Step aside and stand over there. And he stepped aside and remained standing there. And here came the Ethiopian and said, Good news my lord and king. The Lord has judged for you against all who rise up against you! But the king asked the Ethiopian, And young Absalom, is he all right? The Ethiopian said, What has happened to that young man should happen to all my lord the king's enemies who rise up against you.

And the king trembled and went up into the chamber over the gate and wept, as he went and said, My son Absalom! My son, my son, Absalom! If only I had died instead of you, Absalom, my son, my son! They told Joab, Look! The king weeps and mourns for Absalom! And the victory became a day of mourning for all the army when they heard how the king grieved for his son, and the soldiers stole back into the city like soldiers who have fled the battle and are ashamed. But the king covered his face and screamed aloud, My son

Absalom! Absalom, my son, my son. And Joab came into the king's chamber and said, Today you have brought shame to the faces of all your men, who have saved your life and the lives of your sons and your daughters and the lives of your wives and the lives of your concubines, because you love those who hate you and hate those who love you. Today you have made it clear that your officers and men are nothing to you. I can see that if only Absalom were alive and all of us were dead today, that would be fine with you! Now rouse yourself and come out and speak to the heart of your servants. I swear by the Lord, if you don't go to them, not one man will stand by you through the night,

and that would be a calamity worse than anything that has befallen you from your youth until now. And so the king got up and took his seat in the gate. When the army heard that the king had taken his seat in the gate, they all came before the king.

When Israel had fled, each man to his own tent, the people throughout all the tribes of Israel had quarreled with one another and said, It was the king who saved us from the hands of our enemies and rescued us out of the hand of the Philistines, and now he's fled the land because of Absalom. And Absalom, whom we anointed over us, has died in battle. Why do you sit here doing nothing? Why don't you bring the king back? When the king heard what Israel was saying, he sent word to the priests Zadok and Abiathar, and said, Talk to the elders of Judah and say, Why should you be the last to bring the king home to his palace? You're my brothers, my flesh and blood! Why do you want to be the last to bring the king home? And to Amasa say, Aren't you my flesh and blood? May God do this and that and worse to me if I don't make you commander of my army in Joab's stead for as long as you live!

And Amasa turned the heart of the people as if it were the heart of one man, and they sent to the king and said, Come back, you and all your people. And the king turned back and came to the Jordan and the people of Judah had arrived at Gilgal to come and meet the king to lead him back over the Jordan. And Shimei son of Gera, the Benjaminite, from Bahurim, hurried down with all the men of Judah coming to meet the king, and with him came a thousand Benjaminites. But Ziba, the servant of the house of Saul with his fifteen sons and his twenty servants had waded across the Jordan before the king arrived, to help the king's household across and do whatever he needed. But Shimei son of Gera fell down before the king as he was about to cross the Jordan and said, Let my lord not imagine I intended any wrong, and let my lord not remember your servant's offense the day my lord the king left Jerusalem. Let the king put it out of his mind! Your servant knows I have sinned. You see, I'm the first of all the house of Joseph to come down today to meet my lord the king. But Abishai son of Zeruiah spoke up and said,

Why should Shimei not be put to death? Didn't he curse the Lord's anointed? David said, What do I and you have to do with one another, you sons of Zeruiah! Why should any man be put to death in Israel today? Don't you think I know that it is the day on which I have become king of Israel again? And to Shimei the king said, You shall not die, and swore it with his oath.

And Saul's son, Mephibosheth, came down to meet the king and had not cut the nails of his feet or trimmed his beard or washed his clothes from the day the king had gone away to the day of his safe return. And he came down from Jerusalem to meet the king, and the king said, Why didn't you come with me, Mephibosheth? He said, It was my servant, my lord and king. He betrayed me! Your servant told him to saddle me an ass to ride after the king, for your servant is lame. He slandered your servant to my lord the king. My lord the king is like an angel of God: Do with me whatever you please! My father's whole house deserved to be put to death by my lord the king; instead you have set your servant among those who eat at your table. What right have I to cry for more of the king's mercy! The king said, You talk too much, Mephibosheth. I decree hereby that you and Ziba shall divide the property between you. Mephibosheth said, Let him take the whole of it, so long as my lord the king has returned home safely!

And Barzillai the Gileadite came down from Rogelim and crossed the Jordan to see the king on his way. Barzillai was very old—eighty years of age. He had provided for the king while he was in Mahanaim, for he was a man of great wealth. And the king said to Barzillai, Come with me and I will provide for your old age in Jerusalem. But Barzillai said, How many years of life do I have left that I should travel up to Jerusalem with the king? I am eighty years old and can no longer tell good from bad, can't taste what I eat or drink, can't hear the singing of man or of woman. Why should your servant continue to be a burden to my lord the king? Because your servant accompanies the king a little way across the Jordan, should the king reward me with such reward? Let your servant turn back and I'll die in my own city near my father's and mother's graves. Look, here is your servant Chimham. Let him go along with my lord the king and do for him whatever you think best. The king said, Chimham shall go along with me and I'll do for him whatever you think best. I'll do anything you ask of me. When all the army had crossed the Jordan, the king kissed Barzillai and blessed him and Barzillai returned to his home.

And the king went on toward Gilgal and Chimham went with him. And all the army of Judah went with the king and so did half the army of Israel. And now, look! here came all the men of Israel to the king and said, Why have our brothers, the men of Judah, stolen the king away from us and brought the king and his household across the Jordan and led him and his people home to his house? And the men of Judah answered the men of Israel and said, We're nearer kin to the king. Why should that make you angry? Have we eaten a piece of the king? Have we taken a piece of him home with us? But the men of Israel answered the men of Judah and said, Well, we have ten times as many shares in the king, and what's more, it's we, and not you, who're the firstborn! Who are you to look down your noses at us? Weren't we the first to talk about bringing our king home? And the men of Judah talked more hotly than the men of Israel.

∎ ∎

AND there happened to be there a wicked fellow by the name of Sheba son of Bichri, a Benjaminite, who sounded the horn and said, We have no part in David and no share in the inheritance of the son of Jesse. Go home, Israel, every man to his tent. And the men of Israel turned against David and followed Sheba son of Bichri, but the men of Judah stuck by their king and followed him from the Jordan to Jerusalem.

When David arrived in his palace in Jerusalem, he took the ten concubines whom he had left to look after the palace and put them in a separate house under guard, and he provided for them but never went in to them, and they were kept confined, living like widows till the day they died.

Now the king said to Amasa, Call me up the men of Judah, and present yourself with them here three days from today. Amasa went and called up Judah, but he took longer than the appointed time, and David said to Abishai, Sheba son of Bichri will do us more damage than Absalom. You go, take your lord's men, and pursue him before he wins himself fortified cities in which to hide from our eyes. And Joab and the Cherethites and Pelethites and all the warriors followed Abishai out of Jerusalem in pursuit of Sheba son of Bichri. When they arrived at the great rock in Gibeon, Amasa was there before them. Joab wore his tunic belted with a sword strapped against his hip, in its sheath, and as he stepped forward, it slipped out. Joab said, How are you, my brother? And with his right hand he took Amasa by the beard as if to kiss him. Amasa was not watching for the sword in Joab's hand, and Joab struck him through the belly so that his innards spilled upon the ground. He had no need to strike him a second time, and he died, and Joab and his brother Abishai went on in pursuit of Sheba son of Bichri. But one of Joab's young men stood over Amasa and said, Let him who holds with Joab and is for David follow Joab! But Amasa lay rolling in his blood in the middle of the road, and when the man saw the soldiers stop, he moved Amasa out of the road into the field and threw a garment over him, because he saw how everyone who passed by stopped. When he had moved him out of the road, every man followed Joab in pursuit of Sheba son of Bichri.

Sheba passed throughout the tribes of Israel as far as Abel of Beth-maacah, and the Bichrites gathered and followed him. And Joab's men laid siege to him in Abel of Beth-maacah and threw up a mound around the city and battered the ramparts. Joab's men were going to tear down the wall, when a wise woman called out of the city: Listen! Listen to me! Please tell Joab to come here. Come over here so that I can talk to you! They brought Joab over to her and she said, Are you Joab? He said, Yes, I am. She said, Then listen to what your servant has to say to you, and he

said, I'm listening. She said, They used to have a saying in the old days: Ask your questions in Abel, but that, I see, is no longer the custom. I'm one of the peaceful and loyal cities of Israel. Why will you destroy this mother city of Israel and swallow up the Lord's inheritance? Joab answered, God forbid! God forbid that I should destroy or swallow up. You're wrong! There's a man from the hill country of Ephraim and Sheba son of Bichri is his name. He has raised his hand against King David! Hand this one man over to us and I'll leave the city alone. The woman said, Listen, his head will be thrown over the wall to you. And the woman in her cleverness persuaded the whole city, and they cut off the head of Sheba son of Bichri and threw it down to Joab. And he sounded the horn and they left the city and dispersed, every man to his tent, and Joab returned to the king in Jerusalem.

Joab was put in charge of the whole army of Israel, and Benaiah son of Jehoiada had charge of the Cherethites and the Pelethites. Adoram had charge over the slave laborers. Jehoshaphat son of Ahilud was recorder. Sheva was the scribe. Zadok and Abiathar were the priests. And Ira the Jairite too was David's priest.

▪ ▪

AND there was a famine in David's reign for three years, year after year. David asked the Lord, and the Lord said, A blood guilt lies on Saul and on his house, because he put the Gibeonites to death. And so the king summoned the Gibeonites. Now the Gibeonites were not of the stock of Israel, but were a remnant of the Amorites. Israel had sworn an oath to them, but in his zeal for Israel and Judah, Saul tried to destroy them. David asked them, What must I do for you? How can I atone for this sin so that you will bless the Lord's inheritance? The Gibeonites said, We have no interest in the silver or gold of Saul or of his house, nor is it for us to put anyone in Israel to death. But he said, I will do whatever you tell me. The Gibeonites said, Of that man who annihilated us and wanted to destroy and leave us nowhere to live within all of Israel's borders, hand us over seven sons, so that we can hang them before the Lord at Gibeon on the mountain of the Lord. And the king said, I will hand them over. But the king spared Mephibosheth son of Jonathan son of Saul, for the sake of the oath that they had sworn to each other before the Lord—David and Jonathan son of Saul. The king took Armoni and Mephibosheth, the two sons whom Rizpah daughter of Aiah had borne to Saul, and the five sons whom Saul's daughter Merab had borne to Adriel son of Barzillai the Meholathite, and he handed them over to the Gibeonites, who hanged them on the mountain before the Lord, and the seven were put to death and fell together in the first days of harvest, the beginning of the barley harvest.

And Rizpah daughter of Aiah took sackcloth and spread it for herself on a rock. And from the beginning of harvest until the rains poured down out of the heavens down upon the dead, she would not let the birds of the air get at them by day nor the wild beasts by night. They told David what Rizpah daughter of Aiah, Saul's concubine, had done, and he went and fetched the bones of Saul and his son Jonathan from the people of Jabesh-gilead, who had stolen them from the walls of Beth-shan, where the Philistines had hung them on the day they defeated Saul at Gilboa. He brought up the bones of Saul and the bones of his son Jonathan, and he gathered the bones of the hanged men and buried them with the bones of Saul and his son Jonathan in the land of Benjamin in the tomb of Saul's father Kish. After they had done everything the king commanded, God granted their prayers for the land.

• •

AND the Philistines fought another war with Israel, and David and his men went down to Gob to fight the Philistines. And David was tired, and Benob, one of the race of giants, captured David. His bronze spear weighed three-hundred shekels, and he wore new armor. He was about to strike David down, but Abishai son of Zeruiah came to his aid and struck down the Philistine and killed him. Now David's men swore and said, You must not march into battle with us anymore, so that the light of Israel shall not be put out! After this there was yet another war with the Philistines at Gob. That was when Sibbecai the Hushathite slew Saph, another of the race of giants. And there was still another war with the Philistines at Gob, and Elhanan son of Jair* killed Lahmi the brother of Goliath the Gittite, the shaft of whose spear was the size of a weaver's beam. And yet another battle arose in Gath, and there was a giant of a man with six fingers on each hand and six toes on each foot,

* See I Chron. 20:5.

twenty-four in all, and he too was of the race of giants, who mocked Israel, and Jonathan the son of David's brother Shimea slew him. All four of them were of the race of giants in Gath and fell at the hands of David and his men.

▪ ▪

THESE are the words that David sang to the Lord on the day the Lord delivered him out of the hand of all his enemies and out of the hand of Saul, saying, The Lord is my rock, my stronghold, and my deliverer.

And God is my rock in whom I take shelter, my shield, the horn of my salvation, my strong tower and my refuge, my savior who saves me from violence.

I cry to the Lord, who is worthy of praise, and I shall be saved from my enemies.

When the waves of death broke and closed over me, the floodwaters of the netherworld made me afraid. The cords of Sheol bound me; death snared me. In my misery I cried to the Lord. I cried to my God and He heard my voice out of His temple; my scream came to His ears.

The earth shuddered and shook and the foundations of the heavens quaked and shuddered because He was angry. Smoke rose from His nostrils, and a consuming fire out of His mouth; it kindled the living coals.

He bent the heavens and came down; darkness was under His feet. He mounted on a cherub and flew; He was seen on the wings of the wind. He put up tents of darkness around Him, a thickness of cloud, a gathering of the waters.

Out of the brightness before Him, living coals kindled. The Lord thundered out of heaven; the Most High let out His voice. He loosed His arrows to scatter them and His lightning to confound them.

The bedrock of ocean was laid bare, the foundation of the world was uncovered with the Lord's chiding, with the breath of the wind from His nostrils.

He reached down from above and took me and drew me out of the great waters.

He saved me from my strong enemy and from those who hate me, for they were too strong for me.

They came early on the day of my calamity, but the Lord was a staff to me. He snatched me away; He brought me out into the open, because He delighted in me.

The Lord repaid me my righteousness. He rewarded the cleanness of my hands, for I have kept to the Lord's ways and have not wickedly turned away from my God. All his laws have I kept before my eyes; I did not turn from His statutes. I was perfect before Him, and kept myself from sin. Therefore the Lord repays me for my righteousness, my cleanness in the sight of His eyes.

With the faithful You will be faithful; with the perfect You will be perfect. With the pure You will be pure, and cunning with those who are crooked.

You will save the nation that has been humbled, and lower Your eyes upon the mighty to bring them down.

You are my lamp, Lord! The Lord will lighten my darkness. With You I will run down armies; with my God I leap walls.

The way of God is perfect; the word of the Lord is tested and true; He is a shield to all who shelter in Him.

For who is God except the Lord, and who is a rock except our God? God girds me with strength and guides me on my perfect way.

He makes my legs like the legs of a deer, surefooted on the heights. He trains my hands for war and my arms to bend a bow of bronze. You have given me the shield of Your salvation; it is Your battle cry that has made me great.

You have lengthened my stride beneath me and my ankles will not falter.

I will pursue my enemies to annihilate them; I will not return till I have destroyed them. I have destroyed them. I have dashed them in pieces so that they will not rise again. They have fallen under my feet.

You girded me with strength for the battle. You bring those who rise against me to their knees under me. You show me the nape of my enemies' necks so that I can strike those who hate me.

They look for help, but no one is there to help them—even to the Lord, but He does not answer them. Then I ground them as small as the dust of the earth; like the mud I stamped them and mashed them into the street.

And You saved me from strife with my own people, made me ruler over nations. A people I did not know serves me. The sons of strangers cringe before me; their ears hear and obey me. The sons of strangers come in fetters and abase themselves before me.

The Lord lives, and blessed is my rock, and exalted my God, the rock of my salvation, It is God who avenges me and brings nations down beneath me, and saves me from my enemies.

You raise me high above those who have risen against me! You save me from violent men. Therefore I will praise You, Lord, among the nations. I sing praises to Your Name.

He is a tower of salvation to His king and will be faithful to His anointed, to David and his seed forever.

∙ ∙ ∎

THESE are the last words of David, son of Jesse, the man whom God lifted up high, the anointed of the God of Jacob, the darling of the songs of Israel:

The breath of the Lord has spoken through me and His word is on my tongue.

The God of Jacob has spoken to me, the Rock of Israel has said, He who rules men justly, who rules in the fear of God, is like the light of morning when the sun has risen. So stands my house with God! For He has made an everlasting covenant with me, with everything well ordered and secure. He will bring to flower all my salvation and all my desire.

But wicked men are all of them like thistles that have been uprooted; they cannot be taken in hand. He who touches them must have iron and the shaft of a spear in his hand. They must be burned with burning fire where they lie.

∙ ∙ ∎

Now these are the names of David's warriors: Josheb-basshebeth, a Tahchemonite, a chief officer, known as Adino the Eznite, swung his spear and eight hundred fell at one blow.

Next came Eleazar son of Dodo son of Ahohi. He was one of David's three warriors at Pasdammim, where the Philistines gathered for battle and the army of Israel withdrew. He stood his ground and slew the Philistines until his hand tired and stuck to his sword. The Lord brought a great victory on that day: the army turned around and came back for the plunder.

Next was Shammah son of Age the Hararite. When the Philistines gathered at Lehi near a field full of lentils and the army fled from the Philistines, he stood his ground and held the field and routed the Philistines, and the Lord brought a great victory.

And at harvesttime three of the thirty commanders came down to David in the cave of Adullam, and there was a band of Philistines camped in the valley of Rephaim. David was in his stronghold at that time, and the Philistine outpost was in Beth-lehem. And David was thirsty and said, O for a drink of water from the well by the gate of Beth-lehem! And the three warriors broke through the Philistine camp, drew water from the well by the gate of Beth-lehem, and carried it back, but when they gave it to David, he would not drink it, but poured it out to the Lord and said, God forbid that I should do a thing like that! Shall I drink the blood of the men who went and risked their lives? And he would not drink it.

Those were the things these three warriors did: Abishai, the brother of Joab son of Zeruiah, was first among these three warriors. He swung his spear and felled three hundred, and was honored above the Thirty. He became their captain but was never one of the Three.

Benaiah son of Jehoiada was a warlike man from Kabzeel who did great deeds. He slew the two sons of Ariel from Moab. He went down into a pit and slew a lion on a snowy day. He slew an Egyptian, a giant of a man with a spear in his hand. Benaiah went to meet him with a stick and snatched the spear out of the Egyptian's hand and ran him through with his own spear. These were the things that Benaiah son of Jehoiada did. He had a name among the three warriors. He was honored above the Thirty but never became one of the Three. David put him in charge of his bodyguard.

Joab's brother Asahel was among the Thirty and so was Elhanan son of Dodo from Beth-lehem, and Shammah the Harodite, Elika the Harodite, Helez the Paltite, Ira son of Ikkesh the Tekoite, Abie zer of Anathothite, Sibbecai the Hushathite, Zalmon the Ahohite, Maharai the Netophathite, Heleb son of Baanah the Netophathite, Ittai son of Ribai from Gibeah of the Benjaminites, Benaiah the Pirathonite, Hiddai from the wadis of Gaash, Abiel the Arbathite, Azmaveth the Barhumite, Eliahba the Shaalbonite, the sons of Hashem the Gizonite, Jonathan of Shageh, the Hararite, Ahiam son of Sacar the Urite, Eliphelet son of Ahasbai son of the Maacathite, Eliam son of Ahithophel the Gilonite, Hezrai the Carmelite, Paarai the Arbite, Igal son of Nathan from Zobah, Bani the Gadite, Zelek the Ammonite, Naharai the Beerothite, armsbearer of Joab son of Zeruiah, Ira the Ithrite, Gareb the Ithrite, and Uriah the Hittite—thirty-seven in all.

■ ■

AND again the anger of the Lord was kindled against Israel. He incited David against the people and said, Go count Israel and Judah! The king said to Joab and the commanders of the army, Go around among all the tribes of Israel from Dan to Beer-sheba and take a census of the people, so that I will know how many there are. Joab said, May the Lord your God increase the people a hundredfold so that my lord the king may feast his eyes, but why would my lord the king want to do this? But the king's word prevailed against Joab and the commanders, and Joab and the commanders of the army left the king to take a census of the people of Israel. They crossed the Jordan and began at Aroer and the town that lies in the middle of the wadi of Gad, and on toward Jazer, and they came to Gilead and the region of Tahtim-hodshi, went to Dan-jaan and turned toward Zidon. Then they went to the fortress of Tyre and all the cities of the Hivites and the Canaanites and came out in the south of Judah at Beer-sheba. They crossed the whole land and at the end of nine months and twenty days they returned to Jerusalem. Joab gave the king the number of the people who had been counted, and there were eight hundred thousand brave men who drew the sword in Israel, and five hundred thousand in Judah.

Now David was struck to the heart because he had counted the people. David said to the Lord, What I have done is a great sin, Lord. I beg You to take away Your servant's guilt, for I have acted very foolishly. In the morning, David rose, and the word of the Lord came to the prophet Gad, David's seer, saying, Go and speak to David. Say that the Lord says, I give you three choices. Pick which one I shall do to you. Gad came to David and said, Shall it be seven years of famine upon you and your land, or three months of flight from your enemies coming in pursuit of you, or three days of pestilence upon your land? Think it over well. What answer shall I make Him who sent me? David said, I'm in great trouble, but let us fall into the hands of the Lord, for His mercy is great. Let me not fall into the hands of men!

And so the Lord sent pestilence down upon Israel. From morning until noon seventy thousand people died from Dan to Beer-sheba. And as the angel was stretching his hand out to destroy Jerusalem, the Lord was sorry for the evil and said to the angel who was destroying the people, Enough! Put your hand down! The angel of the Lord was standing on the threshing floor of Araunah the Jebusite, and when David saw the angel striking the people, he said to the Lord, Look, It was my sin, I who did wrong; as for these sheep, what have they done? Let your hand fall upon me and my father's house!

And on that day Gad came to David and said, Go up and raise an altar to the Lord on the threshing floor of Araunah the Jebusite. And David went up as the Lord had commanded him through Gad, and Araunah was threshing wheat. He looked up and saw the king and his court coming toward him and fell down with his face to the ground, prostrated himself before the king, and said, Why has my lord the king come to his servant? David said, To buy the threshing floor from you, and build an altar to the Lord, so that the plague that plagues the people will be stopped. Araunah said, Let my lord the king take it and offer it up as he pleases. Look, here are the oxen for a burnt offering, and the threshing sledges and harnesses for wood! I give it all to my lord the king. And Araunah said, May the Lord your God accept it. The king said, No, I will buy it from you at a price. I won't offer the Lord my God burnt offerings that have not cost me anything, and so David bought the threshing floor and the oxen for fifty silver shekels. And there David built an altar to the Lord and offered burnt offerings and peace offerings. And the Lord answered his prayer for the land, and the plague in Israel was stopped.

Now King David was old and well on in years, and though they covered him with cloths, he could not keep warm. His servants said, Let them look for a young virgin for our lord the king to wait upon the king and nurse him and sleep in your arms and keep our lord the king warm. They searched throughout the realms of Israel for a beautiful girl and found Abishag the Shunammite and brought her to the king. The girl was very beautiful. She served the king and nursed him, but the king did not make love with her.

And now Haggith's son Adonijah boasted and said, I'm going to be king! He got himself chariots and horses and fifty men to run in front of him, for his father had never vexed him by asking, Why did you do that? Moreover he was a

very good-looking man and born next in line to Absalom. He conferred with Joab son of Zeruiah and with the priest Abiathar, and they supported Adonijah. But Zadok, the priest, Benaiah son of Jehoiada, the prophet Nathan, and Shimei, and Rei, and David's own warriors did not join Adonijah. And Adonijah sacrificed sheep and oxen and fatted cattle at the stone Zoheleth near En-rogel and invited all his brothers, the king's sons, and all the men of Judah, the king's servants, but he did not invite the prophet Nathan, or Benaiah, or the king's own warriors, or his brother Solomon.

Nathan spoke to Solomon's mother, Bathsheba, and said, Haven't you heard that Haggith's son Adonijah has become king, and our lord David doesn't know anything about it? Come now, let me give you some advice that may save your life and the life of your son Solomon. Go in to King David and say, My lord and king, didn't you swear to your maidservant and say, Your son Solomon shall be king after me and sit upon my throne? Why has Adonijah become king? And, look, while you are still talking with the king, I will come in and back up your words. And Bathsheba went to the king in his chamber. The king was very old, and Abishag the Shunammite attended the king. Bathsheba bowed down and prostrated herself before the king. The king said, What do you want? She said, My lord, you swore to your maidservant by the Lord your God and said, Your son Solomon shall be king after me and shall sit upon my throne. And look! now Adonijah has become king and you, my lord the king, don't know anything about it. He has sacrificed oxen

and fatted cattle and a great many sheep and has invited all the king's sons as well as Abiathar, the priest, and Joab, the commander of the army, but he hasn't invited your servant Solomon. And as for you, my lord and king—all the eyes of Israel are upon you to tell them who shall sit on my lord the king's throne after him. When my lord the king lies down with his fathers, I and my son Solomon will look like traitors.

While she was speaking with the king, here came the prophet Nathan. They told the king, Look, here's the prophet Nathan! And he entered the king's presence and prostrated himself before the king with his face to the ground and said, My lord the king! Did you say Adonijah shall be king after me and sit upon my throne? He went down today to sacrifice oxen and fatted cattle and a great many sheep and has invited all the king's sons and the officers of the army, as well as the priest Abiathar, and they're all there, eating and drinking with him and shouting, Long live King Adonijah! But he didn't invite me, yes, me, your servant, or the priest Zadok, or Benaiah son of Jehoiada, or your servant Solomon! Was this done by my lord the king's wish and without your letting your servant know who was to sit upon my lord the king's throne after him?

And King David answered, Call Bathsheba to come to me! And she came and stood before the king, and the king swore an oath and said, By the living Lord, who has saved me out of every adversity, today I will do as I have sworn to you by the Lord, the God of Israel, when I said, Your son Solomon shall certainly be king after me and shall take my place on the throne.

And Bathsheba bowed down with her face to the ground and prostrated herself before the king and said, May my lord, King David, live forever. King David said, Call the priest Zadok and the prophet Nathan and Benaiah son of Jehoiada to come to me! When they stood before the king, the king said to them, Take your lord's men with you and set my son Solomon upon my mule and lead him down to Gihon. There let the priest Zadok and the prophet Nathan anoint him king of Israel, and sound the horn and shout, Long live King Solomon! Then follow him back here; he shall sit upon my throne and be king in my place, for I have made him ruler over Israel and over Judah. And Benaiah son of Jehoiada answered, Amen, and may the Lord, the God of my lord the king, say Amen as well! As the Lord has been with my lord the king, so may He be with Solomon, and may He make his throne greater than the throne of my lord King David!

And so the priest Zadok, and the prophet Nathan and Benaiah son of Jehoiada, and the Cherethites and the Pelethites went down and set Solomon upon King David's mule and brought him to Gihon. And Zadok, the priest, brought the horn of oil out of the tent and anointed Solomon, and sounded the horn, and all

the people shouted, Long live King Solomon! And the people followed him back up and piped on their pipes and rejoiced with great joy, and the earth quaked with the noise.

Adonijah heard it and so did everybody he had invited, as they were finishing their feast. Joab heard the sound of the horn and said, What's this noise and all this uproar in the city? Even as he spoke, look, here came Jonathan son of the priest Abiathar. Adonijah said, Come in! You're a brave fellow and bring me good news. No, answered Jonathan, and he said, On the contrary, our lord, King David, has made Solomon king. The king has sent the priest Zadok and the prophet Nathan and Benaiah son of Jehoiada and the Cherethites and Pelethites with him and they have

set him upon the king's mule, and the priest Zadok and the prophet Nathan have anointed him king in Gihon and have come back rejoicing, and the city is in an uproar. That's the noise you hear. Solomon is already sitting on the royal throne, and what's more, the servants of the king's court come to our lord King David and bless our lord King David, and say, May your God make the name of Solomon more splendid than your name, and may He make his throne greater than your throne! And the king was on his bed and bowed down low, and what he said was, Blessed be the Lord, God of Israel, who has this day seated my seed upon my throne, so that my eyes can see it. And all of Adonijah's guests trembled and got up and went their ways.

And Adonijah was afraid of Solomon, and he got up and went and clasped the horns of the altar. They told Solomon, Look, Adonijah is afraid of King Solomon. Look, he clasps the horns of the altar and says, Let King Solomon swear he won't kill his servant with the sword! Solomon said, If he proves himself honest, no one shall touch a hair of his head, but let me find any wickedness in him, and he shall die. And King Solomon sent them to fetch him down from the altar, and he came and prostrated himself before King Solomon, and Solomon said, Go home!

∎ ∎

Now the time of David's death was drawing near and he charged his son Solomon and said, I go the way of all the earth. Be strong! Prove yourself a man! Serve in the service of the Lord your God. Walk in His ways. Keep His laws, His commandments, His judgments, and His admonitions as they are written in the Torah of Moses, so that you will prosper in everything you undertake and everywhere you turn, and the Lord will fulfill the promise He made me when He said, If your children take care to walk faithfully before Me with all their heart and with all their soul, you shall never be without a son upon the throne of Israel. Also, you know what Joab son of Zeruiah did to me when he murdered Abner son of Ner, and Amasa son of Jether, the two commanders of Israel's army, shedding the blood of war in time of peace and spilling the blood of war

upon the girdle around his loins and the sandals on his feet. Your wisdom will guide you. Don't let his gray hairs go peacefully down to his grave. To the sons of Barzillai the Gileadite, repay the friendship they showed me in the days in which I fled from your brother Absalom; let them be among those who eat at your table. And look, you have here with you Shimei son of Gera, the Benjaminite from Bahurim, who cursed me with a shameful curse the day I went to Mahanaim. But when he came to meet me at the Jordan, I swore by the Lord and said, I will not put you to death by the sword. Don't let him go free. You're a wise man and will know very well what to do to him that

will bring his gray hair down to the grave with blood. And David lay down with his fathers and was buried in the City of David. And David had reigned forty years over Israel, seven years in Hebron and thirty-three years in Jerusalem.

And Solomon sat on the throne of his father David, and his kingdom stood firm.

THE STORY, CHAPTER AND VERSE

and the same day, of Hophni and Phinehas, as a sign of the downfall of the house of Eli.

3:1   It is a time when visions are rare in Israel. Samuel thinks it is Eli who calls him in the night. Eli understands it is the voice of God and instructs Samuel to listen.   *7*

       God foretells the destruction of the house of Eli. In the morning Eli makes Samuel tell him the Lord's bitter prophecy.

3:19   The child Samuel gains the favor of the Lord and of the people.   *8*

4:1   The Philistines gather for battle in Eben-ezer and rout Israel. Israel returns carrying the ark of the Lord into battle. In their terror the Philistines redouble their efforts, rout Israel, and capture the ark.   *8*

4:12   A messenger brings the news to Shiloh. When Eli learns that his sons Hophni and Phinehas have died on one and the same day and the ark of the Lord is taken, he falls backward off his seat and breaks his neck.   *10*

4:19   Phinehas's pregnant wife hears the news and dies bearing him a son whom she calls Ichabod, meaning, the glory has passed away from Israel.   *10*

5:1   The Philistines bring the ark to the Philistine city of Ashdod and set it beside their god Dagon. The next morning Dagon is found fallen on his face before the ark of the Lord. They set him up again and the next morning he is found in pieces on the threshold.   *10*

5:6   The Ashdodites are afflicted with boils, and the ark is moved to Gath, where young and old are afflicted with boils in their secret parts. They send the ark to Ekron. The people are terrified and summon the princes of the Philistines to demand that the ark be returned to Israel so that God will remove His punishing hand.   *10*

6:1   The priests and sorcerers advise that the ark be placed on a new cart with the images of five golden boils and five golden mice for compensation; that cows whose suckling calves have been taken away from them be yoked before the cart and let go where they will. If the cows take the road and   *12* cross the border into Israelite Beth-shemesh, it will be a sign that the Philistines' affliction has been no coincidence but punishment at the Lord's hand. They do as the priests and sorcerers say and the princes of Philistia observe the cows, mooing as they go, walk straight to Beth-shemesh.

The people are harvesting their wheat and rejoice at the return of the ark. By the great stone in the field of Joshua the Beth-shemeshite, the cows stop. The cart is chopped for wood and the cows are sacrificed to the Lord. The five Philistine princes see it and return home.

6:19	The sons of Jeconiah have failed to rejoice at the return of the ark of the Lord and seventy men are struck dead. The people mourn so great a number of dead and fear the presence of the ark among them. They send messengers to the people of Kiriath-jearim to ask them to come and take the ark away with them.	*14*
7:1	They take the ark to the house of Abinadab on the hill. His son Eleazar is consecrated to its care, and there it remains for twenty years.	*14*
7:3	Samuel urges Israel to return to the Lord and get rid of the alien gods in order not to fall into Philistine hands.	*14*
7:5	Samuel calls Israel to Mizpah and the Philistines gather for battle. Israel calls on Samuel to pray for them. Samuel sacrifices to the Lord who thunders against the Philistines and throws their forces into confusion. Israel pursues them as far as Beth-car. Samuel erects the stone Eben-ezer. Israel recovers its cities lost to the Philistines; there is peace between Israel and the Amorites.	*14*
7:15	Samuel judges over Israel year in, year out from Beth-el to Gilgal and Mizpah, and at his own house in Ramah.	*15*
8:1	Samuel grows old and makes his sons Joel and Abijah judges in Beer-sheba, but his sons bend justice for their own profit.	*15*
8:4	The elders of Israel come to Samuel at Ramah; they want to have a king like all the other nations. The request grieves Samuel. The Lord says that it is not Samuel, it is Himself whom the people have rejected, and He tells Samuel to do what the people say.	*15*

Samuel tells the people the kind of justice to expect under a kingship. But the people want a king to lead them in war like all the other nations.

9:1   Kish of the tribe of Benjamin has a son called Saul.   16

Kish has lost some asses and sends Saul and a servant to look for them. Saul and the servant go through the hills of Ephraim and the land of Shalishah and Shaalim, but they do not find the asses. When they reach Zuph, Saul proposes they go home, but the servant urges him to ask the seer who lives in the town for the right way.

9:11   They meet girls coming out to draw water. The girls urge   17
them to hurry into town and catch the seer before he goes up to the sacrifice. Saul and his servant enter the gates and meet Samuel within the gates.

9:15   The Lord, who foretold Saul's coming in Samuel's ear, says,   17
That is the man! Samuel invites Saul to the sacrificial meal and tells Saul that the asses have been found.

Saul, a member of a small family of the smallest tribe in Israel, is puzzled by this special treatment.

Samuel has the cook serve Saul the pieces of the sacrificial meat that have been set aside for him before his coming.

Saul sleeps on the roof of Samuel's house. Samuel calls him at sunrise and accompanies him on his way. Samuel sends the servant ahead and tells Saul God's intention.

10:1   Samuel anoints Saul and tells him that the Lord has made   18
him ruler over Israel. Samuel foretells that Saul is going to meet two men who will inform him that the asses have been found, three pilgrims who will give him gifts, and a company of prophets who will prophesy in ecstasy, and that Saul will prophesy with them and be a changed man.

10:8   Samuel tells Saul that Saul will go to Gilgal and must wait   18
seven days till Samuel comes to offer offerings to the Lord and tell him what he must do.

10:9   God changes Saul's heart and all the signs come to pass.   18

10:15   Saul tells his uncle all about the search for the asses and the 18
visit to Samuel but does not mention the promise of the kingship.

10:17	Samuel calls Israel to Mizpah, where he rehearses their history, God's goodness, and the wickedness of wanting a king.	*18*

10:20	Samuel arrays Israel before the Lord according to its tribes and clans, and the lot falls upon Saul son of Kish of the clan of Matri of the tribe of Benjamin.	*19*

But where is Saul? God tells them to find him hiding amidst the baggage. Saul stands taller by a head than all the people. They rejoice, crying, Long live the king!

Samuel writes the law of the kingdom in the book.

Saul returns to Gibeah with a following of the faithful, but there is a godless lot of men who mock him and doubt that he is the man who can save Israel from the Philistines.

11:1	Nahash, king of the Ammonites, lays siege to the city of Jabesh-gilead and offers to gouge out every man's right eye and shame all Israel. The elders of Jabesh ask for seven days' reprieve and send messengers for help. The people in Gibeah are weeping at the news when Saul comes home from the fields, walking behind his oxen. Infuriated at the news, Saul hacks the yoke of oxen into pieces, which he sends throughout the land to show Israel what will happen to those who fail to follow Saul and Samuel into battle.	*20*

11:7	A large army from Israel and Judah batters the Ammonites, who scatter so that no two remain together.	*20*

11:12	The people want to kill the wicked louts who had mocked Saul, but Saul wants no killing on this day of victory.	*20*

11:14	Samuel calls the people to Gilgal where they celebrate Saul's kingship anew.	*20*

12:1	Samuel invites Israel to accuse him of any wrong he might have done them. They bear witness to his honest judgeship. He retells Israel's history, Israel's sins, and their tendency to follow false gods, and their punishment at the enemies' hands. Samuel exhorts them and the new king to obey the voice of the Lord.	*20*

Samuel calls upon the Lord to make a miraculous thunderstorm in the midst of the dry harvest season. The people are terrified and ask Samuel to beg the Lord's forgiveness for the sin of wanting a king. Samuel comforts them. He urges them to serve the Lord with all their heart.

| 13:1 | Saul has reigned two years when he picks himself an army of three thousand, keeps two thousand under his command in Beth-el, and puts one thousand under his son Jonathan's command in Benjamin. | 22 |

Jonathan kills the Philistine guard. The Philistines smell revolt, but Saul trumpets the ram's horn throughout the land. Israel rallies to Saul in Gilgal. The size of the Philistine army at Michmas frightens the army of Israel and they run and hide. Some cross over to the enemy. The soldiers who stay with Saul in Gilgal tremble.

| 13:8 | Saul waits the seven days Samuel has appointed, but when Samuel does not come, and Saul's men begin to run away, he offers the burnt offering himself and, here comes Samuel! Saul makes excuses. Samuel foretells that Saul's disobedience to the Lord's command will cost him the kingship. | 22 |

| 13:16 | The Philistines send out three parties of raiders. | 22 |

| 13:19 | There are no smiths in the land of Israel, because the Philistines fear an army of armed Hebrews. Only Saul and Jonathan carry weapons. | 22 |

| 13:23 | A Philistine outpost advances into the narrow pass of Michmas. | 23 |

| 14:2 | Saul is in the outskirts of Gibeah with an army of six hundred men and the priest Ahijah. Nobody knows that Jonathan and his arms-bearer are gone. | 23 |

Jonathan and his arms-bearer make a plan: They will cross over to the Philistine outpost within sight of the Philistines. If the Philistines tell them to stay where they are, they will stay, but if the Philistines tell them to come up, it will be the Lord's sign that He will give Israel a victory.

Jonathan and his arms-bearer kill some twenty men and the terror of the Lord overwhelms the Philistines. At Gilgal Saul observes the commotion in the Philistine camp, calls the roll, and discovers Jonathan's absence.

Saul's army routs the Philistines, and Saul's soldiers who had hidden or gone over to the enemy return and join in the pursuit.

| 14:24 | Saul makes the mistake of vowing that no one shall eat before nightfall. Jonathan, who has not heard his father's vow, | 24 |

tastes a bit of the honey spilling from a honeycomb and his eyes brighten.

Jonathan blames Saul and imagines the greatness of the rout had the army been allowed to eat the plunder.

14:31   The exhausted soldiers sin by falling on the plunder and eating meat with its blood. Saul sets up a stone altar on which the soldiers must slaughter their animals according to the Lord's commandment.   24

14:35   Saul builds his first altar to the Lord.   24

14:36   When Saul asks the Lord if he shall plunder the Philistines, the Lord does not answer him. Saul vows death to the man, even if it is himself or Jonathan, whose guilt has caused the Lord's silence. Saul arrays the army on one side, himself and Jonathan on the other; the lot clears the army. Then the lot clears Saul.   24

The army prevents the execution of Jonathan, the leader of the day's victory.

14:47   Saul's kingship is confirmed. Saul wreaks havoc among the enemies of Israel—Moab, Ammon, Edom, the kings of Zobah, Amalek, and the Philistines.   25

14:49   The sons of Saul are Jonathan, Ishvi, Malchi-shua. He has two daughters, Merab, the firstborn, and Michal.   25

Abner is commander of the army. The war with the Philistines will be long and bitter.

15:1   The Lord remembers Amalek, who ambushed Israel coming out of Egypt. He sends Saul to punish the Amalekites with a sacred massacre: Saul is to kill every man, woman, child, and beast.   25

15:6   Saul sends word to the Kenites, who had befriended Israel, to move away and avoid the Amalekites' doom.   26

15:7   Saul and his soldiers execute the sacred massacre of the Amalekites but take Agag, the king, alive, and spare the best of the animals.   26

The Lord tells Samuel He is sorry He made Saul king of Israel. All night Samuel cries to the Lord. In the morning he goes to meet Saul and accuses him of keeping the plunder for himself, but Saul says that it was the people who spared the best of the animals so as to sacrifice them to the Lord. Samuel teaches Saul that God prefers obedience to the fattest sacrifice. Saul acknowledges his sin.

Samuel refuses to return with Saul because Saul has turned from the Lord's word. When Saul grasps the corner of Samuel's robe, it tears off. Just so, says Samuel, has the Lord torn the kingdom out of Saul's hand in order to give it to a better man.

Samuel has King Agag brought before him and hacks him in pieces.

15:35	Samuel never sees Saul again, but continues to grieve over Saul, because the Lord is sorry He made Saul king of Israel.	27
16:1	The Lord tells Samuel to stop grieving over Saul and to take a horn of oil, go to Beth-lehem, and anoint the new king the Lord has found Himself. Samuel is afraid Saul will kill him if he hears of it, but the Lord tells Samuel to take a young cow and go like someone going to sacrifice, and to invite Jesse the Beth-lehemite. The Lord will let Samuel know whom to anoint.	27
16:6	One after another of Jesse's seven handsome sons pass before Samuel, but the Lord, who sees not as man sees but sees into the heart, has chosen none of them. The only one left is the youngest, a shepherd, out with the sheep. Samuel will not eat till he is sent for. He comes, is rosy-cheeked and handsome, and the Lord says, He is the one! Samuel anoints him in the presence of his brothers. The spirit of the Lord comes upon David and will remain with him from that day on.	28
16:14	The spirit of the Lord leaves Saul, and the Lord's evil spirit makes him afraid. The servants of his court urge Saul to send for the son of Jesse, who knows how to play the lyre and will soothe the king's terrors. David comes to court. Saul makes him his arms-bearer. Whenever the Lord's evil spirit makes Saul afraid, David plays the lyre and the king is comforted.	28
17:1	The Philistines gather for battle on a hill at Socoh in Judah. Saul deploys his forces on the opposite hill. Into the valley between them steps Goliath of Gath, a giant in a bronze coat	29

of mail with a bronze javelin the size of a weaver's beam, and mocks the army of the Lord. He calls for single combat to decide which people shall be slaves, which the masters. The army of Israel trembles before him.

17:12	Jesse the Beth-lehemite is too old to go to war, but his three eldest sons have followed Saul into battle. David, the youngest, goes home to tend his father's sheep.	*29*
17:16	Morning and evening for forty days Goliath stands and mocks the army of Israel.	*29*
17:17	Jesse sends David to carry provisions to his brothers. The battle is pitched, army against army. David finds his brothers, and as they stand talking, Goliath comes and speaks his speech. David hears the frightened soldiers tell each other how rich the king would make the man who killed Goliath and that he'd give him his own daughter for a wife.	*29*

David is outraged that this uncircumcised Philistine dares to mock the army of the living God. David's eldest brother, Eliab, scolds David for his impertinence.

The soldiers tell the king what David is saying and Saul sends for him.

17:32	King Saul discourages young David from attempting to fight the veteran giant, but David says he has killed lions to save his father's sheep and trusts the Lord to save him from the Philistine as well.	*30*

Saul dresses David in his own coat of mail and girds him with his sword, but David cannot walk. He takes off the armor, picks up his stick, puts five stones into his shepherd's bag, and, sling in hand, goes to meet Goliath, who laughs at the handsome shepherd boy. They exchange taunts. Each offers to feed the other's carcass to the birds of the sky and the beasts of the field.

David slings his stone into the forehead of the giant, who falls over dead. David draws Goliath's sword, with which he cuts off the Philistine's head.

The Philistines see their champion is dead and flee. Israel and Judah pursue them to Gath and Ekron.

17:54	David will carry Goliath's head to Jerusalem and puts his weapons into the Lord's tent.	*33*

17:55	King Saul has watched David go to meet Goliath and asks Abner to find out whose son young David is. David is brought before the king and has Goliath's head in his hand. He tells Saul he is the son of Jesse, the Beth-lehemite.	*33*
18:1	Jonathan listens to David and his father talking and comes to love David as he loves his own soul. He makes a covenant with David and gives him his own coat and armor.	*34*
18:5	David does not go home to his father but is made commander in Saul's army. When they return from battle, the women come out of the cities dancing and singing: Saul has slain his thousands and David his ten thousands. Saul, infuriated, thinks, Next thing he'll have the kingdom! From that day on Saul keeps his eye on David.	*34*
18:10	The next day, when God's evil spirit comes upon Saul and David plays the lyre, Saul has his spear in his hand and tries to pin David to the wall. David leaps out of the way. Saul becomes more and more afraid of David because the Lord has turned away from Saul and toward David. Saul sends David into battle, but David is more and more successful because the Lord is with him. Saul sees that all Israel and Judah love David.	*34*
18:17	Saul offers David his older daughter Merab to wife if David will fight Saul's battles, because Saul hopes the Philistines will kill David for him. But Merab is given to be the wife of Adriel the Meholathite.	*34*
18:20	Saul learns that his younger daughter Michal loves David. Saul asks for a bride price of one hundred Philistine foreskins, but David is not killed. He counts out two hundred Philistine foreskins to the king and is given Michal to wife.	*34*
19:1	Saul wants Jonathan and the servants of his court to kill David, but Jonathan loves David. Jonathan and David make a plan: David will hide in a field where Jonathan will bring his father, praise David to him and discover if David is in danger. Jonathan recounts to the king the many services David has done him. Saul vows that David shall not die. Jonathan	*35*

brings David back to the king, and David serves Saul as before.

19:8	Another war and David routs the Philistines. The Lord's evil spirit comes upon Saul. Saul has his spear in hand; David plays the lyre. Saul tries to pin him to the wall. Twice David leaps out of the way. The spear sticks in the wall, and David flees.	*35*
19:11	Saul sends his messengers to David's house, but Michal lets him down through the window, puts the household idol into David's bed, and tells the messengers David is ill. Saul sends the messengers back to bring him David, bed and all. Under the blanket, with a goat's-hair wig, the messengers find the idol. Saul is angry at his daughter's treachery. She tells him that David threatened to kill her.	*35*
19:18	David flees to Samuel in Ramah. Saul sends his messengers to seize David. Saul's messengers meet Samuel leading a group of prophesying prophets. The spirit of God comes upon Saul's messengers and they prophesy too, and so do Saul's second lot of messengers, and so do the third. Saul goes to Ramah himself and God's spirit comes upon him, and he prophesies also, and he lies naked all day and all night.	*36*
20:1	David flees to his friend Jonathan, who assures David of his love and protection. David and Jonathan plan a test: during the feast of the new moon David will hide out in the field where Jonathan will let him know what the king says when he misses David from his place at table.	*36*
20:24	The first night the king assumes a ritual uncleanness keeps David away. The second day he asks for him. Jonathan says David has gone home to sacrifice with his brothers in Bethlehem. Saul becomes furious, abuses Jonathan, and accuses him of treason. Doesn't Jonathan know, he asks him, that David endangers Jonathan's kingship? He throws his spear at Jonathan, who leaves in anger and humiliation.	*37*
20:35	Jonathan and David make a plan by which Jonathan will let David know whether to return or flee for his life. Jonathan comes into the field where David is in hiding and shoots an	*37*

arrow and shouts to the little boy he has brought with him to run and find the arrow on the farther side, and to hurry. The boy, suspecting nothing, is sent back to town.

David comes out of hiding. The two friends, weeping, renew their mutual covenant and David flees.

21:1	David, without companions, food, or weapons flees to the priest Ahimelech at Nob. David tells Ahimelech he is on urgent business for the king. The priest supplies him with sacred show-bread to eat and Goliath's sword for a weapon.	*37*
21:8	The Edomite Doeg happens to be there on that same day.	*38*
21:11	David leaves King Saul's domain and flees to King Achish of Gath. He is recognized and pretends to be a madman.	*38*
22:1	David hides in the cave of Adullam, where his brothers come to him. A band of some four hundred discontents gather around David in his exile.	*38*
22:3	David asks the king of Moab for asylum for his father and mother.	*38*
22:5	The prophet Gad sends David to Judah.	*38*
22:6	In Gibeah, Saul sits, spear in hand, surrounded by the servants of his court, whom he accuses of keeping David's whereabouts hidden. Doeg, the Edomite, says he has seen David in Nob. The king sends for the priest Ahimelech and all his kin. Doeg is the only one of all Saul's servants willing to kill the eighty-five priests of Nob. Doeg massacres the inhabitants of the city of Nob. Only Abiathar escapes and joins David's band.	*38*
23:1	The Philistines attack Keilah. The Lord sends David to save Keilah. Saul sees a chance to take David and his men inside the walled city. David has Abiathar ask the Lord if Saul means to destroy Keilah, and if Keilah means to hand David over to Saul. The Lord says yes on both counts. David and his six hundred men leave quickly.	*39*

23:14	David and his men live in the wilderness of Ziph. Saul searches for him day in, day out.	40
23:16	Jonathan comes to the woods to encourage David's trust in God. He says that King Saul knows that David will be king of Israel and Jonathan will be second to him. They renew their covenant.	40
23:19	Certain Ziphites come to tell King Saul that David is hiding in the woods. Saul thanks them and asks them to discover David's exact location and situation.	40
23:24	In the Arabah David hears that Saul is coming and goes down one side of the crag as Saul comes around the other side of the mountain. Saul is about to encircle David when a messenger calls him away to fight a Philistine attack.	40
24:1	Returning from the battle, Saul learns David is in En-gedi, and pursues David with three thousand picked men.	41
	Saul goes to relieve himself inside a cave in the back of which sit David and his men. David's men urge him to kill his enemy, whom the Lord has delivered into his hands, but David will not harm the Lord's anointed.	
	He blames himself for cutting off a corner of Saul's coat. David calls after Saul, prostrates himself, and shows Saul the corner of his coat.	
	Saul acknowledges David's goodness, his own sin, and obtains David's oath that after he is king he will not wipe Saul's name off the face of the earth. Then Saul returns home, and David and his men climb back into their mountain stronghold.	
25:1	Samuel dies. Israel mourns, and buries him in Ramah.	42
	David moves into the wilderness of Paran.	
	Nabal, a bad rich man, is celebrating his sheepshearing in Carmel. David sends his young men to him with a friendly greeting, reminds Nabal of the protection that he gave Nabal's shepherds in the wilderness, and asks him for a share of the feast. Nabal refuses rudely.	
	David is on his way to kill Nabal and all his household but is intercepted by Nabal's beautiful and clever wife, Abi-	

gail. She comes bringing presents of food and wine and words of praise and respect. She urges David to leave vengeance to God.

The next morning, when Nabal has slept off his drunkenness, Abigail tells him what has happened. Nabal lies there like a stone. Ten days later he is dead.

David sends for Abigail to be his wife.

| 25:44 | Saul gives David's wife Michal to Palti. | 44 |

26:1   The Ziphites inform Saul that David is on the hill of Hachilah. In the night David and Abishai steal into Saul's camp. David prevents Abishai from killing the anointed king where he lies asleep surrounded by his sleeping soldiers. They carry off the king's spear and water jug. David stands on the opposite hill and taunts Abner.   44

Saul recognizes David's voice and asks his blessing.

27:1   David and his two wives and six hundred men and their families escape to Achish, king of Gath, who gives them the town of Ziklag in which to live.   46

27:9   When David raids Geshurite, Gizrite and Amalekite towns, he massacres man, woman, and beast to cover his tracks, telling King Achish that it is the towns of Israel he has raided. King Achish is persuaded David will be his slave forever.   46

28:1   When the Philistines gather for battle against Israel, Achish includes David's men among his forces and makes David his bodyguard.   46

28:3   King Saul has banished the sorcerers from the land, but the size of the Philistine army terrifies him. Saul disguises himself, seeks out the wise woman of En-dor and calms her fear of entrapment, but when he asks her to raise Samuel up, she understands that he is the king.   46

Samuel foretells the death, in the coming battle, of Saul and his sons, and the end of his dynasty because he failed to execute the Lord's command to massacre the Amalekites.

Saul falls full-length upon the ground. The woman insists that he eat and regain his strength before he leaves.

29:1	Achish has to send David and his men home to Ziklag because the Philistine princes fear treason from David, who has killed his ten thousands of Philistines.	48
30:1	When David and his men arrive in Ziklag, they find it has been raided and set on fire. Their wives and children have been taken captive. In their grief his men threaten to stone David, but the Lord tells them to pursue the band of raiders. Two hundred of his men are tired and stay at the wadi of Besor. An Egyptian slave leads David and his four hundred men to the band, who are enjoying their plunder. David and his men recover every one of their women and children and take much booty. David insists on sharing the spoils with the two hundred men who stayed behind with the gear.	48
30:26	David returns to Ziklag and sends shares of the enemy's spoils to the Israelite cities.	50
31:1	The Philistines rout the army of Israel. Saul and his sons are killed. Saul is dying with an arrow in his belly and begs his arms-bearer to kill him before he falls into the enemy's hand. When the arms-bearer refuses, Saul falls on his own sword. His arms-bearer kills himself.	50
31:7	Israel flees, and the Philistines occupy the deserted cities. They strip Saul of his armor, hang it in the temple of Ashtoret, and cut off his head and hang his corpse on the wall of Beth-shan.	50
31:11	A band of warriors from Jabesh-gilead travel through the night to take down the corpses of Saul and his sons and bury them in Jabesh-gilead.	50
II SAMUEL 1:1	Three days after David's return from the battle, a young Amalekite comes to Ziklag and tells a story of having killed the dying Saul at his request. He brings David Saul's crown and bracelets. David commands his men to kill the regicide.	50
1:17	David mourns and laments the death of Saul and Jonathan and sings the Song of the Bow.	53

3:28	David's public mourning demonstrates his innocence in the death of Abner. David curses the house of Joab for the killing of Abner.	*56*
4:1	Ish-bosheth loses heart; Israel is frightened.	*56*
4:4	Saul's son Jonathan has a son who was lamed in both feet when his nurse dropped him in the panic flight that followed the news of Saul and Jonathan's deaths. The son's name is Mephibosheth.	*57*
4:5	Rechab and Baanah, two commanders in Saul's army, kill Ish-bosheth in his house during his midday nap. They bring Ish-bosheth's head to David in Hebron. David has them killed, as he killed the Amalekite who hoped to be rewarded for the killing of King Saul.	*57*
5:1	The tribes of Israel come to Hebron and make a covenant with David before the Lord. They anoint David king over Israel. And now David is king of both Judah and Israel.	*57*
5:6	David marches against the Jebusites in Jerusalem. They taunt him, saying that the blind and the lame could prevent his entry.	*57*
I CHRONICLES 11:6	David captures Jerusalem. Joab, first over the ramparts, becomes commander of David's army.	*57*

II SAMUEL 5:9	The stronghold is named the City of David, and David builds a city around it.
	    Hiram, king of Tyre, sends David what is needed to build him a palace of cedarwood.
	    David's power and kingship is established.
		57

5:13	David takes more wives and concubines. The sons born to David in Jerusalem are Shammua, Shobab, Nathan, Solomon, Ibhar, Elishua, Nepheg, Japhia, Elishama, Eliada, and Eliphelet.	*58*
5:17	The Philistines gather against the new king, but the Lord breaks through them like a torrent of water.	*58*

| 5:22 | The Philistines return and the Lord attacks them from the thorn trees. | *58* |

| 6:1 | David and his people come to fetch the ark out of the house of Abinadab. They set it on a new cart, which they lead down the hill. When the oxen stumble, Abinadab's son, Uzzah, reaches out his hand to steady the ark. The Lord kills him on the spot. | *58* |

| 6:8 | David is angry and afraid to have the ark brought into the City of David. He diverts it to the house of Obed-edom the Gittite, where it remains for three months. David hears about the blessings that the presence of the ark bestows on the household of Obed-edom, and goes to fetch it. | *58* |

David brings the ark of the Lord into the City of David amidst song and dance, and they sacrifice at every sixth step a fatted calf.

Dressed in a priestly linen robe, David turns and whirls with all his might. Michal, looking out of the window, sees and despises him. After the sacrifice is shared among every one of the people, David goes home to bless the palace, but Michal comes out to attack him with her bitter words, saying that he has exposed himself before his servants' slave women. David defends his willingness to dance and lower himself before the Lord, who has made him ruler in the place of Michal's father, Saul.

Michal remains childless as long as she lives.

| 7:1 | The Lord gives David rest from his enemies. | *60* |

David wants to build the Lord a house. The Lord gives His answer through the prophet Nathan: The Lord recalls how he has accompanied Israel through the wilderness without requesting a house for Himself. It is the Lord who has built David a house, and planted Israel in a place safe from the malice of their enemies. The Lord promises that after David's death He will love and punish David's descendants like a human parent.

| 7:18 | David answers the Lord and remembers his own littleness, which the Lord has exalted. He thanks the Lord for revealing the future to him and prays the Lord for His great Name's sake to do what He has said. | *61* |

8:1   David subdues the Philistines definitively.   62

     David defeats the Moabites, makes them lie down on the ground, and with a cord measures off those who are to live and those who are to die. The Moabites become David's vassals and pay him tribute.

     David defeats Hadadezer, king of Zobah, and the Arameans of Damascus who come to his aid. David sets up garrisons in Aram Damascus and the Arameans become David's vassals. David brings the golden shields of Hadadezer's men and the copper from their cities to Jerusalem.

     Toi, king of Hamath, sends his son Joram with presents.

     David sanctifies the plunder from Edom, Moab, the Ammonites, the Philistines, and Amalek.

     The Edomites become his vassals.

8:15   David brings law and justice to all his people.   62

     David's cabinet consists of Joab, the commander of the army, Jehoshaphat the recorder, Zadok and Ahimelech the priests, and Seraiah the scribe. Benaiah has charge of the Cherethites and the Pelethites. David's sons serve as priests.

9:1   David sends for Jonathan's son Mephibosheth, the only one 63
left of the house of Saul to whom David can show friendship for Jonathan's sake. David restores to Mephibosheth his grandfather Saul's inheritance and gives him Saul's servant Ziba to serve him and cultivate his land. But Mephibosheth himself is to stay in Jerusalem and eat every day at David's table.

9:12   Mephibosheth has a son, Mica.   63

10:1   The king of the Ammonites, who has been friendly to Israel, 63
dies. David sends envoys to console his son Hanun, but the princes of Ammon persuade Hanun that the envoys are spies. Hanun shames David's envoys by cutting their beards and skirts.

     David sends the envoys permission to stay away till they are fit to be seen, and prepares for war.

     The Ammonites call upon their allies, the Arameans from Beth-rehob and Zobah, and the kings of Maacah and Tob.

     Seeing himself outnumbered, Joab divides his forces between himself and his brother Abishai so that each can come to the other's aid.

When the Arameans are put to flight, the Ammonites flee too.

The Ammonites send for help from Shobach, the commander of Hadadezer's army. Israel defeats and kills Shobach. The vassal kings under Hadadezer make peace with Israel and become Israel's vassals.

The Arameans will no longer come to the Ammonites' aid.

11:1   In the season in which kings march to battle, David sends   64
Joab and the army to conquer Rabbah while he remains in Jerusalem. One evening he rises from a nap, and as he walks up and down the palace roof, he sees a beautiful woman bathing. It is Bathsheba, the wife of Uriah the Hittite. David sends for her and makes love to her. She goes home and sends David word that she is with child.

David sends for Uriah the Hittite, who is fighting with Joab's army. David questions Uriah about the progress of the siege and sends him home to his wife. But Uriah the Hittite will not sleep with his wife while the army of the Lord is sleeping out in the field. He sleeps with the soldiers at the gates of the palace. David has him stay another night and gets him drunk, but again Uriah sleeps at the gates of the palace. In the morning David sends Uriah back with a letter to Joab saying, Put Uriah in the front lines so that he will be killed.

Joab sends Uriah to fight close to the city walls where several warriors are killed. When Joab sends the king a report of the action, he teaches his messenger what to do if the king gets angry: The messenger must say, Uriah the Hittite is dead too.

After Bathsheba's mourning is over, David takes her to be his wife.

12:1   What David has done has angered the Lord. He sends the   67
prophet Nathan to tell him the story of the ewe lamb: A rich man with many flocks and herds has a visitor to entertain. Unwilling to slaughter one of his own animals, he takes the pet ewe lamb of a poor man. What the rich man has done angers David. He says, A man who does such a

pitiless thing deserves to die. Nathan says, You are the man! The Lord will take your wives and give them to one of your own house to do in the eye of the sun what you have done in secret. David says, I have sinned against the Lord! Nathan says that David will not have to die; it is the son whom Bathsheba bears him who must die.

12:16   David begs God for the child's life. His servants cannot get the king to eat or to rise from the floor and are frightened to tell him when the child dies. David sees them whispering and knows and rises off the floor and eats.   68

   David consoles Bathsheba. She bears him his son Solomon.

12:26   Joab subdues the city of Rabbah and sends for the king to accomplish the capture in his own name. David gains the crown, and a large booty, and makes the people work as slaves, and so he does in every captured Ammonite city.   68

13:1   David's son Amnon falls in love with his beautiful half sister Tamar. His clever cousin Jonadab devises a plan: Let Amnon feign sickness and have the king, his father, send Tamar to cook him a healing dish.   69

   As Tamar is serving him, Amnon clears the room of his attendants, entices Tamar into his bedroom, and violates her. Afterward he turns her out of doors. Screaming in her shame, Tamar goes to live a desolate life in her brother Absalom's house.

   King David is angry but fails to punish Amnon, his firstborn.

13:23   Two years later Absalom invites the king and the king's sons to his sheepshearing. The king refuses but is pressed to let the princes go with Absalom. Absalom instructs his servants to kill Amnon at his signal. The king's sons mount their mules and flee.   70

   At a rumor that Absalom has slain every one of the king's sons, David tears his clothes in mourning, but cousin Jonadab says that it is only Amnon, whom Absalom had planned to kill from the day he violated Tamar.

   The watchman on the gate sees the princes coming down the road.

   Absalom flees to Geshur.

14:1	Joab sees that David has consoled himself for the death of Amnon and misses Absalom. He sends for a wise woman from Tekoa, instructs her to dress herself in mourning, and tells her what to tell the king. The woman of Tekoa asks the king's help: She says her family wants to kill her one surviving son because he killed his brother in a quarrel. The king promises to save her son's life. Now the woman draws the analogy with the king's own exiled son. The king guesses the hand of Joab in the matter, and sends Joab to bring Absalom home, but will not see him face-to-face.	72
14:25	Absalom is admired for his flawless beauty. His hair weighs two hundred measures by the royal standard.	*73*
14:27	Absalom has three sons and a beautiful daughter, Tamar.	*73*
14:28	Two years after his return Absalom summons Joab to send him to plead with the king. Joab does not come. Absalom sends for Joab a second time, but he will not come. Absalom has his servants set Joab's barley field on fire. Joab comes to complain and Absalom sends him to plead for him with the king. The king agrees to see Absalom, and kisses him.	*73*
15:1	Absalom provides himself with chariots, horses, and fifty men to run in front of him. He stands in the road and sympathizes with his father's subjects who are coming to the king for judgment. If only he were judge, says Absalom, he would see justice done. He touches and kisses people and turns the heart of Israel toward himself. Four years pass. Absalom asks the king's permission to fulfill his vow to serve the Lord in Hebron. Absalom sends spies to the tribes of Israel: Israel must shout, Absalom has become king in Hebron! David's counselor Ahithophel joins the growing conspiracy.	*73*
15:13	David urges his court to flee Jerusalem, leaving ten concubines to look after the palace. The king halts by the last house to watch the Cherethites, the Pelethites, the Gittites, and the six hundred men from Gath as they march past.	74

He tells Ittai the Gittite, himself an exile, to stay with the new king, but Ittai stays with David, whether to live or to die.

The land weeps as king and army pass the Kidron Valley toward the wilderness.

15:24   The Levites bring the ark, but David sends it home to Jerusalem.   *74*

David sends back Zadok and Abiathar, the priests, and their sons Ahimaaz and Jonathan, so that they can let the exiled king in the wilderness know what's going on at court in Jerusalem.

David walks barefoot and weeping up the Mount of Olives.

15:32   Hushai the Archite comes to join his friend David, who sends him back to Jerusalem to frustrate Ahithophel's counsel and help Zadok, Abiathar, and their sons.   *75*

16:1   Ziba, Mephibosheth's servant, brings provisions for the exiles, but Mephibosheth has stayed in Jerusalem thinking that he is about to gain his grandfather's kingdom. The king endows Ziba with Mephibosheth's inheritance.   *75*

16:5   In Bahurim, Shimei of the house of Saul curses David and throws things at him. David will not let Abishai kill this mouthpiece of God's ill will against David.   *75*

Arrived at the Jordan, the king and his exhausted people rest.

16:15   In Jerusalem Absalom questions the loyalty of David's friend Hushai. Hushai answers that his loyalty belongs to his friend's son Absalom, whom Israel has chosen for its new king.   *76*

16:20   Absalom seeks Ahithophel's trusted counsel. Ahithophel counsels Absalom to go in to his father's concubines before the eyes of Israel, and tents for this purpose are pitched on the palace roof.   *76*

17:1   Ahithophel counsels that he fall, that same night, upon the tired and distraught David, kill him alone and bring the army home to the new king.   *76*

But Hushai argues that the king is too good a soldier to

be so caught out, that a rumor of Absalom's early failure might disperse the army. Hushai counsels that Absalom call up the entire army of Israel and lead it to the battle himself.

The Lord, who intends Absalom's destruction, causes him to take Hushai's counsel.

17:15	Hushai sends the news via Zadok and Abiathar to their sons waiting near a well in En-rogel. A boy sees and betrays them to Absalom, who sends his people to find them. Ahimaaz and Jonathan hide inside the well; the woman of the house covers the well under a mound of grain. Absalom's people fail to find them and return to Jerusalem. The two men climb out of the well, find the king, and tell him to hurry his people to the far side of the Jordan.	77
17:23	Ahithophel sees his counsel has not been taken and goes home and hangs himself.	77
17:24	Absalom puts Amasa in charge of the army. Amasa's father has lain with Joab's mother's sister.	77
17:27	David arrives in Mahanaim. Shobi, Machir, and Barzillai bring him beds, dishes, and food.	77
18:1	David divides his army into three parts, puts a third under the command of Joab, a third under Joab's brother Abishai, and a third under Ittai the Gittite. The army begs David not to risk himself in the battle; he stays by the city gates.	77
18:5	The soldiers hear King David command the commanders not to hurt Absalom. The battle is fought in the forest of Ephraim. Absalom's hair gets caught in the branches of an oak. His mule walks away from under him. Joab thrusts three lances through Absalom's heart; Joab's ten arms-bearers beat him to death. Joab sounds the horn and ends the battle. Absalom's body is thrown into a pit and covered with a pile of stones.	77
18:18	Absalom had erected himself a monument called Absalom's Memorial.	79
18:19	Ahimaaz asks to carry the good news to the king; Joab prevents him and sends an Ethiopian. Ahimaaz insists on going also and overtakes the Ethiopian.	79

David sits between the gates. When the watchman reports a man running, David promises himself good news. The watchman recognizes Ahimaaz and reports a second man running, and still and again the king insists the news is going to be good.

Ahimaaz arrives. He congratulates the king on the defeat of his enemies. Asked about Absalom, Ahimaaz says he saw a great commotion as he was leaving without knowing what it was. The king asks him to step aside and questions the Ethiopian, who brings the same news. Asked about Absalom, he says all David's enemies should end up like Absalom.

19:1	The king howls with grief for his dead son, and the victory turns into a day of mourning.	*79*
19:6	Joab comes to the king and accuses him of caring more for his rebellious son than for the army that has saved his life and kingdom. He foresees calamity if the king allows the army to disperse. David rouses himself and meets his soldiers at the city gate.	*80*
19:10	The tribes of Israel and Judah quarrel and blame one another: What shall they do now? Who shall go to fetch the king home?	*80*
19:12	The king sends Zadok and Abiathar to urge the elders of Judah to fetch him home to his palace. He promises his kinsman Amasa the command of the army in Joab's place. Amasa turns the people's hearts back toward the exiled king. The king arrives at Gilgal, where the men of Judah meet him and lead him back across the Jordan.	*81*
19:17	Shimei would like to be the first, but Ziba and his sons and twenty servants have already waded across the Jordan to assist the king's return. Shimei begs the king to forget the curses with which he cursed him in Bahurim. Abishai offers to kill Shimei, but the king vows to let him live.	*81*
19:25	Mephibosheth hurries to meet the king and, to demonstrate his grief at the king's absence, has not cut his beard or	*81*

washed his clothes. He swears he told Ziba to saddle a horse for him so he could join the king! He throws himself on the king's mercy. The king divides the inheritance between him and the loyal servant Ziba.

19:32   Barzillai crosses the Jordan to meet the king. Barzillai is eighty years old and refuses the grateful king's invitation to be his pensioner in Jerusalem, inviting the king to confer his intended kindness on Chimham.   *81*

19:41   All the army of Judah and half the army of Israel accompany King David across the Jordan. Israel and Judah quarrel over who is to be first with the king.   *82*

20:1   The scoundrel Sheba son of Bichri turns the people of Israel against David, but the people of Judah stick by him and return with him to Jerusalem.   *82*

     David confines the ten concubines, whom he had left to look after the palace, in a state of widowhood for the rest of their lives.

20:4   The king commands Amasa to call up the army of Judah and return within three days. Amasa does not return by the appointed time. David sends Joab and Abishai to pursue Sheba before he can fortify himself inside a walled city.   *82*

     They meet Amasa by a rock in Gibeon. Joab steps forward to kiss Amasa and pierces Amasa's belly with his sword.

     Everyone who passes stops to look at Amasa's innards spilling onto the road until a man moves him and covers him up.

     Sheba has reached Abel of Beth-maacah. Joab besieges the city and is about to destroy it, but a wise woman persuades the city to cut off Sheba's head and throw it out to Joab, who returns to the king in Jerusalem.

20:23   Joab has charge of the army; Benaiah has charge of the Cherethites and the Pelethites. Adoram has charge over the slave laborers. Jehoshaphat is recorder, Sheva is scribe, and Zadok and Abiathar are the priests. Ira is the priest of David.   *83*

21:1   There is famine in the land. David asks the Lord, and the Lord says it is because of the blood guilt of Saul, who had   *83* put to death the Gibeonites with whom he had made a covenant. David asks the Gibeonites what he must do to satisfy them, and they ask not for gold and silver but for seven sons of the house of Saul.

The king spares Jonathan's son Mephibosheth, but hands over Rizpah's two sons Armoni and Mippibaal, and the five sons Saul's daughter Merab had borne to Adriel the son of Barzillai.

The Gibeonites hang them on the mountain before the Lord.

21:10	Rizpah spreads sackcloth on a rock and keeps the birds and beasts off the bodies from the beginning of the harvest until the coming of the rains. David fetches the bones of Saul and his son Jonathan from Jabesh-gilead and buries them together with the bones of the seven hanged men. The famine passes from the land.	*84*
21:15	Another war with the Philistines. David is tired; the giant Benob captures him. Abishai saves David. The army persuades David not to go into battle again. In yet another war Sibbecai slays Saph, another giant. There is still another war and Elhanan kills Lachmi, Goliath's brother. In another battle in Gath a giant with twenty-four fingers and toes mocks Israel, and Jonathan, the son of David's brother Shimea, slays him.	*84*
22:1	On the day the Lord delivers him out of the hands of his enemies and the hand of Saul, David sings to the Lord.	*85*
23:1	David speaks his last words.	*86*
23:8	David's warriors are named and ranked and their exploits are remembered.	*86*
23:13	Once when a band of Philistines camped by the cave of Adullam, David thirsted for water from a well by the gate of Beth-lehem. Three warriors broke through the Philistines to bring water to the king, who refused to drink what had been brought at the risk of the warriors' lives. He pours the water out before the Lord.	*87*

23:18	David's thirty warriors are listed and include Uriah the Hittite.	*87*
24:1	The Lord is angry with Israel and incites David to send Joab and the commanders to make a census of the men of Israel and Judah, against Joab's advice. At the end of nine months and twenty days they return to Jerusalem and report that there are eight hundred thousand soldiers in Israel, and five hundred thousand in Judah.	*88*
24:10	David acknowledges the sin of counting the Lord's people. The prophet Gad brings David the choice of three punishments: seven years of famine, a three-month flight from a pursuing enemy, or three days of pestilence. David chooses the last punishment, preferring to put himself in the hand of the Lord instead of in the hand of man. Seventy thousand from Dan to Beer-sheba die between morning and noon and the angel stands on the threshing floor of Araunah stretching his hand to destroy Jerusalem, when the Lord says, Enough! David begs the Lord to punish him and his house and not the people. David buys Araunah's threshing floor and builds an altar to the Lord. The plague ceases in Israel.	*88*
I KINGS 1:1	King David is old; he cannot keep himself warm. They find him a beautiful virgin called Abishag the Shunammite to take care of him. The old king does not make love to her.	*89*
1:5	Haggith's son, Adonijah, announces he is going to be king. Joab, the commander of the army, and the priest Abiathar support Adonijah. The priest Zadok, Benaiah, the prophet Nathan, Shimei, Rei, and David's warriors do not join Adonijah. When Adonijah sacrifices near En-rogel, he invites the king's sons and the men of Judah, but not Nathan, or Benaiah, nor the king's warriors, nor his brother Solomon. Nathan advises Solomon's mother, Bathsheba, to tell King David that he promised her he would make Solomon king. Nathan comes to back her up. David sends Zadok, Nathan, and Benaiah to anoint Solomon. When Adonijah's guests hear the joyful commotion, they	*89*

flee. Adonijah clasps the horns of the altar and refuses to leave.

Solomon swears not to kill him if he behaves himself.

2:1   The time has come for David to die, and he charges Solomon to be strong and to serve the Lord and keep His commandments in order to ensure the continuance of his dynasty in Israel.   93

2:5   He tells him not to let Joab go unpunished for the murder of Abner and Amasa, to repay Barzillai for his friendship during the insurrection of Absalom, and not to let Shimei get away with having cursed the king in Bahurim.   93

2:10   David dies and is buried in the City of David.   93

Solomon sits on his father's throne. The kingdom stands firm.